YOU ARE AN *Abundant* BABE

Skyrocket your self-belief, integrate the secrets to success, and tap into the abundance that's meant for you.

VIOLA HUG

ISBN: 9781799002123

DEDICATION

This book was written for you. The ambitious and persistent human. The one who will live out her huge goals, and make an even bigger impact. Everything you desire is on its way to you, and I am so grateful you are here and allowing me to be a part of your journey upwards.

I love you.

My heart pounds with love and pride as I also dedicate this book to my Father, Hans Joachim Hug. The official launch date of this book being my Dad's birthday (March 11th), it makes everything about this book and this journey more powerful. Although he lost his life so young, I am grateful for the passion it ignited in my soul, and for the drive I now have to wake everyone up and encourage them to live a life they love. My Dad is no longer here, but he's influenced a legacy that will impact millions.

CONTENTS

ACKNOWLEDGMENTS

I firstly want to thank my husband, Nick. For the catalyst that made me see I had a purpose not only in this lifetime but one that will impact generations. For being my editor-in-chief, laughing at my jokes, and celebrating this journey with me.

To my Mom, Conny, who always support me on my path to living out my purpose, and believes in me whole-heartedly.

To my coach Melanie Ann Layer, who holds me to a higher standard, helps me amplify my impact, and creates the space for me to grow and calibrate to her level, and beyond.

To my friend, Tiffani Purdy, who's ambitious action and get-it-done attitude gave me the push to finally write this book, and get it done in just a handful of months.

To my clients, current and to come, whom I love to pieces and are living proof that you truly can achieve it all in life.

To my internet friends, who I love so much and have encouraged me more than I could ever have imagined.

To the Universe, my guides, and my higher-self, for supporting me through it all in life and constantly reminding me of my power.

Finally, in the words of Snoop Dogg, "I want to thank me for believing in me. I want to thank me for doing all this hard work, I want to thank me for having no days off, I want to thank me for never quitting, I want to thank me for always being a giver and trying to give more than I receive. I want to thank me for trying to do more right than wrong, I want to thank me for just being me at all times."

HOW TO MAKE THE MOST OF THIS BOOK

Each chapter includes a heck of a lot of magic, as well as applicable action steps, journaling prompts, and "soul work," as well as "integration space" to take notes and journal.

In order to *really* receive the messages you are meant to from this book, read each chapter with an open mind and beginners' mindset. This means regardless of whether you have heard the content before, or something similar, read it as if it's the first time you've ever read it. If you notice yourself thinking "I know this," that's a mega cue to re-read it and apply the beginners' mindset. Pro-tip: when we say "I know" we are actually telling our subconscious mind it does not need to pick up new information, and we close ourselves off from learning. The life-changing magic is in between everything you "know," so pay close attention.

Each chapter includes a "soul work" prompt on something you can immediately apply to start integrating what you are learning; solidifying the new energetic and mental pathways that are forming to support your most abundant self. Actually *do* the work, and pay attention to when you are resisting an exercise - this probably means your soul is in desperate need to practice it. After all, education and inspiration are nothing without application.

At the end of each chapter (with some additional bonus pages at the end), you will find an "integration space." This is a space for you to journal and record everything from your "soul work" prompts. I also encourage you to use it to note down any "aha-moments" you have while reading the chapter. Aha-moments are like a mind-blown moment. A moment in which you perceived something in a new way, it really impacted you, or something you really want to remember and apply.

This book is your guide, your journal, your side-kick for channeling your true abundant self. Feel free to highlight, draw, underline, journal, and intentionally doodle on the pages. Truly make this copy your very own, unique version.

All my love, Vxx

Foreword

It gives me immense pleasure to write this foreword. Everything about this book, from the information to the way it was written and published, says so much about Viola. She is a woman whose courage is one of the boldest I have ever known. As one of her mentors, I have had the opportunity to have a front row seat to witness her success unfold. I have had the privilege to watch her as she overcame every challenge she faced. Viola leads herself consistently so her clients and readers feel safe to follow in her leadership.

I remember when Viola first declared she was going to write this book. I could tell by the certainty in her voice that I would be reading her pages sooner than I could even imagine! She sat in front of her computer in different countries around the world and let the words pour out of her. Every week, on our calls, she would tell me how close she was to the finish line. Hours of writing, the editing, the artwork for the cover, the formatting....her heart and soul went into every aspect of the book and it has been a tremendous honor to watch it come together. Viola is the real deal!

In this book you will gain incredible insight and learn in the most beautiful way from a woman who paves the path of a life of her own creation every day. She leads a life most dream of: the freedom to travel the world, a strong, committed marriage, a thriving podcast, and clients who adore her. She IS the abundant babe she teaches about, and through her words you will experience what it feels like to embody your greatest life.

Viola,

Thank you for being a shining example for what is possible for womankind.

I love you, so will they.

XO

Love Always,

Melanie Ann Layer

ALPHA FEMME

From me, to you
YOU CAN HAVE IT ALL

It was not uncommon for me to be referred to as a dreamer, the one with a wild imagination, and the one who spends too much time making up stories in her mind.

As much as that sounds like it would be a compliment now, beyond the words I felt the condescending tone in the voices of my teachers, parents, elders, and peers.

When I was 4 years old and drew a millionaire princess in a castle as my "what I want to be when I grow up" picture, I received a pat on the head and was told that wasn't a real job.

When I was 11 years old and started a pop band with my bestie, I got glared at by my peers and told to focus on things that mattered by my elders.

When I was 17 years old and applied to universities where I could chase my dream of being a world-famous actor, I was encouraged to look into something that would offer me a stable future instead.

When I was 21 years old, and I shared my list of "future-husband-must-have-traits," I was mocked by my classmates and told that this sort of person doesn't exist.

When I was 23 years old and decided I would start a business rather than pursue a career with the degree I graduated with, I was lectured on responsibility and told I was "throwing my life away."

But I couldn't help myself. I almost enjoyed peoples shocked reactions to my crazy goals. I loved sharing my ideas, and I was never too 'put off' by peoples reactions. In fact, it was often a source of fuel for me in my early days. I wasn't too bothered by other peoples opinions, because I felt like I knew a secret they didn't.

When I look back on my life now, I feel like I had always known there is something special within me, and that other people just couldn't see it yet. My journey back to abundance proved to me it was possible, and along the way, it also showed me just how unique, gifted, and special you are too. Yes, you, reading this. You are special. You are meant for big things. You are innately abundant. **You will have it all**.

But you already know that, *don't you?*

Some names in this book have been changed to protect the identity of the individuals, however, all examples given are my perspective of real peoples situations.

Introduction
THE MAKING OF THIS ABUNDANT BABE

When I was just a child I already knew I was going to do fantastic fucking things with my life. I knew it in my soul, I just didn't know what it would look like. But I felt this inner energy, this calling, that reassured me I would have my cake *and* be able to eat it too. With second servings.

Now, just like anyone else, I was raised by people in a society that is designed to shoot down your desires, create false idealisations of what "success" looks like, and have limiting beliefs pressed upon you since before you could even speak – about yourself, your power, money, relationships, sex, health, and worthiness. So, for the most part, this encouraging voice inside of me stayed small.

She came out to play when I was being artistic, whether it was writing books, stories, poems, or songs, painting, or playing. She whispered in my ear when I was doubting myself, she had witty comebacks (only in my mind) when people smirked at my goals or wild perceptions of life.

Now, as much as I was born to be someone, life knew part of my purpose was to help others believe in themselves too, so it served me up a shit-show and a million reasons to doubt myself along my path. Don't get me wrong, I am hashtag grateful AF for my life, and all I have been through, and the eternal optimist in me often didn't even let me experience my own pain in its entirety.

I remember the first time I really doubted myself. I was 11 years old and life was fucking fantastic. I was part of my school's 'Spice Girls' band (I was Posh Spice, until Ginger Spice left and I got demoted to Sporty Spice). Even when I moved schools, no bother, I just started my own band with my new bestie (The Sweet Strawberries). I was in ballet AND karate, I was in the school choir AND was making plans to perform our bands original (complete with killer choreography) in front of the whole school. I got cast as lead in our community play, and met the coolest girl ever who became my BFFE (the E stands for "ever", we thought forever was 2 words...) - I was HIGH on life, I wanted it all, and it was mine for the taking.

You're probably thinking right now, "oh em gee you were so cool, how did you doubt yourself?" In sequence, here is what happened. At our school's choir performance, performing Celine Dion's "My heart will go on," parents made comments about how easy it was to spot me because I always overemphasized my mouth movements as I sang. Next, in our kitchen, my friend and I were performing our song and dance moves in preparation for our live performance, in front of my parents and a family friend, when the family friend broke out into laughter saying how cute it was that I did all of my dance moves way bigger than the others. When my friends came over to play, I was told not to take charge so much, as it would make me look bossy.

Here's the thing. I have *always* been over the top. I have *always* been a leader. I have *always* been a little quirky. And I have *always* had big ass ambitions. I LOVE that about me (now...) I love that who I am is so big and bright that it inspires some to keep going, and it triggers others to explore themselves more. Either way, it's helping people step closer into who they're meant to be. I don't have to be anyone I'm not to make that happen, I just have to be 100% who I am meant to be. I know this both intuitively and because it's written in my astrology and human design charts #bornthisway.

As an 11 year old, I felt amazing about being me, and it's honestly the last time I remember feeling that way for at least another 14 years. Because those comments, although meant innocently, made me doubt myself. They made me question my brightness. They made me, for the first time, consciously dim my light. And it didn't turn back on for wayyyy too long.

At this moment in time, something massive happened. I went from having a deep knowing about my inner epicness, to feeling like I needed someone out in the world to validate it for me. Maybe I wasn't so shit-hot? Maybe I'm not meant to be a movie star, a singer/ songwriter, an inventor, and philanthropist (I'm kidding myself if I think I knew what that word meant back then, I even had to google it just now to make sure it's what I meant... Yes, even someone who stutters when pronouncing big words can write a book, you're welcome). So I looked outside of myself for proof of how awesome I am, I looked for validation, and I tried to achieve things that would prove my worth. This was one of the biggest mistakes I've ever made, yet something I heartbreakingly see far too often in my friends, family, and clients.

The next few years of my life introduced the more 'ugh' parts of my teen years, which I'm sure we've all been through in one way or another. I was bullied for being the "new girl", an ongoing theme - as I went to 13 different schools because we moved around so much. And not only because I was new, but I was weird, I wore second-hand baggy clothes, and my parents were foreigners. I became extremely aware of my underdeveloped body (helloooo, super later bloomer here), and compared myself against the "women" around me. At age 14, I was forced to grow up in a way I never expected. And at age 16 the trajectory of my life was forever changed.

Unknowingly, at the age of 16, a seed was planted in my soul, and a fire lit in my heart. It would take me almost 6 years to learn how to turn this drive into purposeful action, and I would have to go through a lot of hurt to find myself along the way. But through this time I decided this for sure:

I wanted it all. I was not willing to settle for mediocrity in any aspect of my life. I wanted the fulfilling career, passionate relationship, the freedom to do what I want when I want, travel, nice home(s), money, lots and lots of money (shout out to all my fellow one-day-to-be-billionaires), to live in luxury, experience life's diversity, and give freely – All. The. Things.

I wasn't going to stop until I achieved all of the above, and when I did, I would keep going in inspiration to serve others, give back, and keep growing.

And now, more than ever, I believe part of my journey was to discover that this inner knowing I had that I was meant for greatness, is something we all have. I am fiercely determined to crack you wide open and inspire you to take a real look at yourself. I will believe in you until you have the courage to believe in yourself, in hopes that your journey comes with more ease than it did for me, and that all of the challenges you go through are embraced with a kind and ambitious heart.

I will take you through how you can move from looking for the answers to your desires out there in the world, like I did for way too many years, to finding them inside of yourself. How you can cultivate unshakable self-love and self-belief so your journey forwards is not in wonder of whether or not you will achieve your greatness, but in appreciation of the journey to an inevitable outcome. I will take you deep into the making of this Abundant Babe, and share with you the teachings, perception shifts, and practices *you* can embody to also become the most Abundant Babe you know. Everything I share is from my experience and perspective, and I hope to shake things up for you just the right amount, so you can take what feels good, take what is needed, and apply it into your life.

This book is for the visionary. The one who desires abundance in all areas. The one, who like me, is interested in creating fulfillment and abundance as a whole person, in a holistic way, and having it all with second servings, please.

Abundance is your birthright. Your visionary goals will

come true. Synergy creates magic. Energetic alignment creates physical mastery. Growth is a journey to be embraced. High vibes and a positive outlook will change the world. Vibrant health is our default state. Integrity and credibility are a given. Success manifests in your life with ease.

You are an Abundant Babe.

One
IT'S TIME TO WAKE THE FUCK UP

If you found out you were dying how would you show up in life? What new things would you want to experience? What would you do differently? Well, friend, you are dying. We all are. – Nick Taylor (my hubs)

It's funny how life passes you by. A thought that surfaces almost more frequently than "I'm hungry," is "where has the time gone." Time flies. If I were to ask you to remember what you ate for breakfast on June 13th, 2008, unless something pivotal happened for you that day, your response is probably something like, "I can't even remember what I had for breakfast today!" Why is that? Well, most of us go through life unaware and unattached. You move through life letting things happen to you, complaining about them to your friends, always looking ahead waiting for a Friday, hoping that you'll be happier when you get there. Spoiler alert: you won't be (unless you makes some major changes).

Then there are the memories that linger in your brain. The ones you were really there for. The ones that impacted your emotions at a level that penetrates so deep you can feel it for decades to come. Whether it was your family vacay, Christmas as a kid, your first heartbreak, or your babies' first steps.

For me, one of my most life-changing memories happened 14 years ago. It was a Sunday morning, and the rain was pouring down outside. I was so grateful to be inside where it was warm and cozy. It was a rare occasion where the whole family was getting along. Between my 16-year-old rebellious self, my 11-year-old sister's awkward early teens, and my 4-year-old sister's "threenager" attitude, it was safe to say we were a bit of a handful for (what we referred to her as back then), my pushover Mom. (She's honestly one of the strongest women I know to have dealt with mine and my sisters' strong personalities, and harsh teenage years). But not this morning. We'd had breakfast together and played board games together. Just after midday, we decided to snuggle up on the couch and watch a movie – the Incredibles. Unknowingly what was awaiting me was one of the most defining moments of my life. One of the moments that pulled forth my passions and ignited a fire in my soul. It was at that moment, I heard my mom's voice yell down from the top of the stairs, "Dad's dead".

It was that Sunday afternoon I learned what it was like to lose someone you love.

It was that Sunday afternoon that I realized we don't

live forever.

And it changed my perspective on life for good. Not that I knew it at the time. It took me into a deep state of denial, depression (with a cocktail of other mental health issues), and amplified the validation I thought I needed. I went into a spiral of self-harm, drinking too much, taking drugs off strangers, waking up with broken bones, falling for any man that looked my way (can you say, Daddy issues?! Yes you can, real loud), to doing anything I could to punish myself for the pain I thought I deserved to feel, and hating myself for the way I acted. And this went on for 5 years.

It took me all the way to the point where I no longer saw a reason to be alive, for me to wake the fuck up.

Although, many of my memories of this time are a blur, this is another memory I can distinctly remember.

It was 2010, and I was embarrassed because I had lashed out at my flatmates over a matter that was definitely not lash-out-worthy. I was embarrassed beyond belief with some happenings between my ex-boyfriend and his new girlfriend. My family had moved out of New Zealand (where I was living and studying), which had me feeling abandoned. I was at university, which as you may know, brings upon its own kind of pain. Before you think, "wow you must have had your shit together by now, being at university and all." No. No, I didn't have my shit together. I pretty much just lucked out that I ended up studying something I was actually interested in. But, I only went because my ex decided to "do something" with his life, rather than just party every single night of the week. So I followed him 14 hours south of where I lived to be a grown up too.

I felt like no one really understood me or cared for me at all. I was ashamed of who I was. Unexcited about the future. And my mind was living in some super dark places. I was thinking about all the reasons why I had failed at life, why I didn't deserve to live, and how I was really just a burden anyway. I felt completely alone in the world. And for all I knew, I would always be.

It was a random weekday afternoon when I was doing some grocery shopping. As per usual, I was trying to stretch my $10-20 budget as far as I could make it go when suddenly all I could feel is cold. A sense of numbness swept over my entire body. It was as if I had no thoughts, yet my mind was on overdrive. In what felt like hours, but in reality was probably only a couple of seconds, I stood there, staring into the freezer at a supermarket. I suddenly couldn't finish my grocery shopping, because I couldn't really see the point. I couldn't see the point of completing this mundane task when I couldn't really even see the point of living any longer.

I wanted to take my own life. I didn't want to live in this deep pain I felt any longer. *I hated being alive.*

I stood there, the cold frosty air spilling from the freezer, cooling me down; totally disconnected from myself and the world. During this deep moment of pain, I felt a gentle and nurturing wave pry its way into my body. It was this feeling that told me, with absolute certainty, "you're not done here yet". It was a little bamboo seed planted deep in my soul. A little seed of hope. It was that little voice inside of me returning after so many years of me ignoring her sweet sound.

I don't really know where it came from. All I know is it saved my life. Because it was in that moment I decided I would fight for my life, and I would ask for the help I needed.

For so long my light had been getting dimmer and

dimmer. It was this moment, and the times that followed, that reminded me of all I had inside of me. As I started to realize this, I started to dream again. I started to let these big goals slip out of my mouth, and I even welcomed the snickers of others, with a little smile on my dial, because I KNEW a little secret. I knew I was meant for big fucking things in this world, and I was not going to stop until I had it all.

As I sit here in my Airbnb, traveling the world as a digital nomad with my beyond perfection soulmate husband by my side, with a booming online soul business, the best relationships with people all over the world, getting inboxed messages of how I have changed peoples lives, and completely and utterly in love with my life, **I am certain, without a shadow of a doubt, that no matter where in life you are, or where in life you have been, a life that is more magical than you can even imagine awaits you**.

Looking back now with 20/20 vision, I know what it was all for. All the downs, and all the ups. I know why I had to go through these experiences. I'm often caught in a state of awe and wonderment about how magnificent our universe really is, and how every experience we have in life is really happening *for* us. Losing my Dad at such a young age was such a painful experience, however, it lit a passion in me to understand and KNOW true health (cue: one Bachelor of Science in Human Nutrition + 10 years of additional self-study, courses, and working in the industry). It lit a desire to know how to live a fulfilled life now, and it planted a seed that grew in me like Chinese bamboo, simmering under the surface for years, before exploding up into the sky.

Quick side story in case you've never heard of how Chinese bamboo grows, let me enlighten you. Once it is planted it needs a shit ton of nurturing and support -

water, nutrients, fertile soil, and sunshine. And for the first year of caring for the plant daily, you see nothing, not even a little sprout above the soil. The same continues for the second, third, and fourth year. Right now you're probably wondering; Is the seed dead? Is it even doing anything? Is this worth it? This so often happens with our dreams and visions for ourselves too. We nurture and pursue what we want, but just because we can't see an immediate shift or an inevitable goal line, we wonder if anything is really, truly changing. Trust me, it is. Because in the fifth year of nurturing the Chinese bamboo, it finally sprouts, and continues to grow up to 80 feet tall (24 meters) in JUST 6 WEEKS! Cool, huh!? (Side note to the side note: you are the Chinese bamboo, don't you **dare** stop nurturing your dreams).

So, back to what I was saying. I share this story of losing my Dad and the apparent turmoil that followed with you for one main reason; Had I not gone through these experiences, I may have never learned the true value of life. Too many people wait for something terrible to happen to them, or to someone they love, before they do something about their health, goals, relationship, you name it. Listen to me closely: you DO NOT need to wait for an external shift to push you into this realization. You can choose to make the shift you desire *now*.

You do not need a degree first (okay, in some very rare cases you need a degree), you don't need to clean your house, you don't need anyone's permission. If you have a desire that is pulling at your heart strings, the time to act is now.

If you need a further perspective shift, know that there are 151,600 people who die every single day. The fact that you woke up this morning means you still have a purpose; act like it. As I said, too many people wait for something major to happen in their lives before they make a change, but the magic is that you don't have to wait at all. You can choose right now to start acting in gratitude of the life you have, and in positive anticipation for everything that is to come for you.

Understand this, the universe is on your side when it comes to your soul purpose. In fact, the Big U has probably been dropping hints for you left, right, and center, even before you picked up this book (hello checking the time at 11:11, triple-numbers galore, synchronicities in conversations, the rainbow, the feather, the penny on the ground, and seeing the post on Facebook of what you were literally just talking about). The universe is constantly guiding you and supporting you on your life path, and is really here to make the process a whole lot easier for you... unless you are not paying attention.

This is why there are so many stories of people having an awakening after a tragic life experience, a sickness in the family, suicide attempt, an addiction, near death experience, or other traumatic event. When you are not listening, the universe will find a way to keep sending you more and more obvious signals to get on track with your purpose. You can either take action now, or wait until you're pushed into it (which can happen in a massive way as I mentioned before, or when you've been unsatisfied for long enough that you have no choice but to change).

This is why I am so grateful for the experience I had with my Dad at such a young age. It completely jolted my life and gave me a perspective that some people don't get until it's far too late. I appreciated this perspective, and that it stirred something within me, but it took me deciding I would take my own life before I really got set on the right track. I think, in hindsight, I would have never dared to go through with the dark thoughts I had, but they scared me enough to knock some serious sense into me. The universe had finally jolted me awake, and I was ready to get my mind, and life, back together.

Here is the cold hard truth gorgeous: it's time to wake the fuck up. It's time to stop living life as if you have forever. And remember; every decision you make in the now will become a memory you'll have to look back on forever. You can either look back in regret and with heaviness, or when you're old and grey, feel the corners of your mouth curl upward as you think to yourself, "wow, I really did live. What an epic effin' life."

Soul work: *Take some time to journal and reflect on pivotal moments in your life. Make one list of things you are incredibly proud of and that you are grateful for, and another list with experiences that taught a lesson, paying close attention to what you learned, and how you can positively utilize these in your life now, and moving forward. Remember, none of it is bad, it's all happened for you, and I love you.*

INTEGRATION SPACE

Two

BEYOND THE COMFORT ZONE BUBBLE

Life shrinks or expands in proportion to one's courage. – Anais Nin

I know what you're thinking. It's *all well and good to say "go for your dreams," but it's a hell of a lot easier said than done.* It's a scary shit show out there, and you have limiting beliefs, self-sabotage, lack of skill, and a whole heap of other reasons that make it hard for you; perhaps even harder for you than for other people.

Sorry, Susan, I'm not falling for this. I label all of the above under non-valid excuses. It's not that all of these things are actually holding you back, it's that you don't fully understand how this whole "*go after your dreams*" thing works - so let me enlighten you.

You have probably heard of the comfort zone analogy before, how all good things happen outside of your comfort zone, but are you really aware of how to navigate through it?

To understand how the whole concept of comfort zones, growth, intuition, and following your desires works, you have to understand some basic principles. Firstly, we, as humans, are infinite. Meaning we have unlimited potential. We are having a human experience; meaning we experience polarity, and we are (only) limited by our perceived restrictions.

When we come into this world, many of us quickly forget the magnificence of who we are at our core and create stories about what we are capable of based on our environment and our experiences. On top of that, one of our traits of being human means we have a subconscious aspect of our mind, referred to as the ego, whose only job is to keep us alive for as long as possible, and during that time procreate as much as possible. The ego only cares about comfort and safety. It doesn't care that you are an infinite soul, it doesn't care about your dreams, desires, or that you want to have a fulfilling life. And as it is for most people, the ego is the dominant energy in your mind.

I know the idea of "comfort" over freedom sounds like an absolute nightmare for any modern day visionary (I mean, I straight up gag), but here is the bottom line - if you die you're definitely not going to have the chance to fulfill those dreams you have (in this lifetime anyway)! So the ego and it's whole "keep you alive" thingy is *kinda* important, you just have to learn how to navigate past the boundaries the ego has set for you.

What makes it into your comfort zone? Great question! Anything that your ego decides is safe for you - that is anything that doesn't threaten your primitive survival needs - safety, shelter, food, love, and acceptance (so you're not abandoned from your tribe). The interesting thing is that we as humans have evolved a lot quicker than our primitive ego could keep up with. Meaning? The human stress response is actually designed to protect you from life or death situations - not to protect you from traffic jams, money troubles, public speaking, or family drama that you get stressed out in our mind about. However, as smart and magnificent as the human body really is, this stress response can't tell if you're stressed about an upcoming job appraisal, or if there's a jumbo lion about to eat your head off. The same goes for fear - are you scared to tell your parents you are starting a business, or has an enemy tribal army just invaded your village?!

On top of that, the ego is a little scaredy-cat. ANY time you try anything new, it will automatically decide it can't be any good for you. *I mean* ***really*** *Brenda, you're staying alive just fine... You wake up in the morning and snooze exactly 3.5 times, get up and go for a pee, look at yourself in the mirror and say a few self-deprecating comments to keep you in line with this lifestyle, zombie your way over to the coffee machine,* and so on, *until you cuddle up back in bed at night and your mind decides to suddenly remember the 150 tasks you forgot to do today, and every time you did anything slightly embarrassing.* We *got this shit on lockdown, why would you want to change?!* The ego doesn't really get the picture that every time you try something new, your life isn't necessarily in danger. It can learn new tricks and install new programs, but only after massive repetition and/or heightened emotional stimulation.

The other interesting thing is that when we take action towards our true desires, the fears and thoughts that flood our mind are not random. They are actually the habits, patterns, thoughts, beliefs, and perspectives that have kept us where we are in that particular area of our life. Some big Life-changing things to remember are; If you really desire something, it is meant for you. When you take action anyway, these fears will dissipate. Your life is not really in danger when it comes to soul-fulfilling activities, and when you listen to your intuition and follow divine guidance, you are giving more power to this - and the ego's grip on you loosens.

You see, in case you didn't know, here's how it all goes down. The soul communicates to you through good feeling things, like inspiration, hope, desire, and possibilities. The ego communicates to you through fear, doubt, shame, and other 'low vibe' thoughts or feelings. So when you feel a deep desire about something, it is not random. Let me repeat that in bold so you really get it.

When you desire something, it is meant for you.

That's how it works. There is NO way we were designed to desire things that weren't within our souls potential. Like, *wow, I would love to be an author/[insert anything else you desire] one day... HA Jokes on you Debbie, you want it, but you could* NEVER *be an author.* No. Just no dude, that is NOT how the universe works. If you desire something, it is meant for you, and you can undoubtedly 111 billion zillion gazillion percent achieve it - If. You. Choose.

Here's the catch. Yes, you can achieve it. But if you don't already have it in your life, it means it is out of your comfort zone. This means that if you want it, you're going to have to get uncomfortable, and consciously make the decision to move out of your comfort zone, despite the fears the ego will undoubtedly present.

You have to make this decision with your conscious mind (the 5% you have access to), and be bold, brave, and courageous, as 95% of your subconscious programming, a.k.a. your autopilot response, a.k.a. your ego, presents you with the 437 reasons you could never do the thing. The power of this is that if you can remember these words when you are next in this position (which I believe is just around the corner for you, *you ambitious babe you*), you will have the power to not only make the decision to be courageous in that moment but also to be consciously aware of exactly what beliefs or patterns have been holding you back from calling that into your life.

If you notice your first thought is, "what if I run out of money," you've got some money mindset work to do.

If your next thought is, "what if people don't take me seriously," it's time to work through your fear of judgment or the opinions of others.

If you notice after you say you will do it, suddenly **everything**, including decluttering your desk, becomes a priority over taking bold actions towards your goals, time management, procrastination, and putting yourself at the bottom of your priority list needs to be addressed.

You see; you live within our comfort zone bubble. Your desires that allow you to grow are beyond your comfort zone, and the border of your comfort zone is made up of all of these fears, beliefs, habits, etc., that have kept you where you are. As you move towards your goals, you are made aware of anything that needs to shift in order for you to truly step into the next version of yourself.

It's not an easy path to completely flip this response to fear, but I can promise you, with awareness and conscious action, you can push through, and your intuitive soul guidance will magnify.

Take this example, and one of the biggest leaps I have ever made out of my comfort zone. To paint the picture for you, it was early 2012 and I had just finished my Bachelor of Science, with a double major in Human Nutrition, and Sport and Exercise Science. Sounds super fancy, I know - you'd think I would be in a super cool job after 3.5 years at university, but nope. I had learned the cold, hard truth that so many 21st century tertiary educated students face: a degree does not equal a career. So instead, I was paying the bills working in retail. I felt a little better about myself because I was "third in charge," which I thought made my situation a bit less sad... which it didn't really. Third in charge? At a men's clothing store? Basically, it just meant I got to tell staff to fold t-shirts while both of my bosses were on yet another smoke break (do all non-smoking employees get punished by not getting 101 extra 5-minute breaks a day)?! Anyway, I digress.

Around the same time I started working in this job, I had also started my first business in the Network Marketing industry. It was a company whose values really aligned with my own holistic health outlook on life, I was genuinely a fangirl of the founder, and I had seen my Mom using their products for 5+ years at this point. So when I couldn't get a job in my field, I desired freedom SO deeply, and loved this company, I knew it was the right decision to partner with them. Now, my intuition guided me to this decision, however, my desire was so strong that I wasn't really bothered about all the fears that may normally consume someone starting something new like this. Maybe I was naïve on what it would take, or maybe I just saw it as my ticket out of the rat race, but either way, I wasn't really that impacted by the fact I was stepping outside of my comfort zone at this point. It wasn't until a few months later when I had **yet again** been declined leave by my boss at my job, and had to miss another commitment to my friends (that meant more to me than this flipping job), when my boss said something to me that was my "it's over, rover" moment. As I begged for the day off so I could go and see my friend before she was moving overseas (indefinitely), he said: "you have to care more about your job than your personal life." UM. HELL FREAKING NO, BRO!

In that moment I KNEW I had to quit that job. This time, it was scary. Although I had started that business a couple of months ago, I hadn't really done anything. I had no proof it would work, and between my at-the-time-boyfriend-now-husband's part-time job, and our living expenses, we really did rely on my full-time income. But I was SO OVER being an employee. I was never designed to be one. I had the trait of being a hard worker, so I always gave my all in a job, but I resented it. My soul was tired, and I was just not fulfilled with the idea of someone else deciding when I could go pee, how much I earn, or when I'm allowed to eat, *I need more than one 30 min break a day Karen, I get hangry, okay?!* (Later in life, discovering my Human Design would confirm why I am like this #disruptor).

The idea of being self-employed and being able to earn my own income at my own pace excited the heck out of me (Clue #1: The soul is capable of this). I was absolutely convinced that I was going to do big things in my life, and I squealed with excitement about the fact I was about to REALLY step into that place. I was only mildly concerned about how we would pay our bills, if my friends would judge me for my career choice, or if my boyfriend Nick, and my Mom, would support me. When I made the internal decision I was scared, but I also trusted in my soul and believed in my potential, and I couldn't wait to tell Nick and Mom. Little did I know, this is where my fears would magnetize.

The exciting news quickly turned into a debate, which escalated to a full-on, me-sobbing-my-eyes-out "*I thought you believed in me*" drama show. Cue: Mine and Nick's first ever, and only 'real', fight. They brought up all of the fears I had been ignoring within me. *What if it doesn't work, what if you can't pay your bills, how is it going to work, isn't it more logical to replace your income and then leave your job.* (Clue #2: Basic, non-life threatening, pretty irrational but seemingly serious fears emerging? You're on the right track).

Hearing their concerns about my decision only impacted me the way it did because deep down, these fears that they were projecting on to me were also my own fears. Now naturally, in my very non-emotionally-intelligent way, I flipped out. I cried, I hid in a corner, I yelled at them, I said they didn't care about me, gave Nick the silent treatment the whole way home (which he did not respond well to).

In all fairness, I know why they reacted this way too, and let this be a lesson for you too. Firstly, there is the aspect of them projecting their own fears, but there is more to it than that in this scenario - I had never given them a reason TO believe in me. Sure, we think "but they LOVE me, they have to believe in me"... *but umm girl, you're telling me you wanna go lead a team to 7 figure success and you're crying in a corner right now 'cause one person questioned you? Tell me again how you're gonna do that?!* Firstly, the people closest to us have often seen *all* of us. In our empowered states, sure, but most likely more of you when you're hangry (it's a real thing, okay), that time you freaked out because your sister took your top without asking, or how you fart around with no pants on half the time (and hey, that last one ain't so bad). They have probably seen you talk a big game and flake out 10 minutes later more than you can count, they've witnessed you make bad financial decisions (*but those shoes were buy one get one HALF off*), and other questionable life decisions. How are they to know that this time you really mean it?

Anyway, this fight that Nick and I were having had only lasted for about 5 minutes after we got into bed, (where I had abruptly made a blanket border between us), when I felt Nick's hand scooch over to my side of the bed as he rolled over and whispered, "I think you should quit your job". Needless to say, the fight was over.

Funnily enough, when the decision was made I was going to quit my job, the fears starting setting in stronger. I'm not sure whether it was the one personal development book I had read by then (*Think & Grow Rich* by Napoleon Hill, in case you're wondering), or my stubbornness, or my desire to be rich and free that kept me going, but I chose to act in spite of my fears, and every action I took towards that decision, made the fears seem less big (Clue #3: As you take actions, fears dissipate).

After I had left my job, it only took me about 7 weeks to cover our additional business expenses, and about 6 months to replace the income I was making in my job. (Clue #4: I was able to do it, it *was* meant for me). It goes without saying, Nick and my Mom were on my team by then, and haven't really questioned my business, investment, or life decisions much since.

Listen, sister; intuition is the REAL DEAL. It speaks through you all of the time, and you have to remember its cues if you want to be supported on your divine life path. When we start to understand that essentially none of our thoughts are even our own, it begins to make WAY more sense. *Say whatttt? My thoughts are not my own? Whatever do you mean, Viola?*

I'm glad you asked. Yes. Our thoughts are not our own. We are essentially a neutral ground between the battles of our ego and soul. Like I mentioned earlier in the chapter, we are either being influenced by thoughts coming from our ego or from our soul/higher self/higher guidance/God/the Universe (you get the picture). The more you listen to your ego, the stronger its' commands become, not only for you - but collectively. As everyone is becoming more hashtag woke, which basically just means learning to trust their inner guidance and connection to the ultimate source, we begin to give more power back to the divine - both individually and collectively. So you honoring your intuition, following that gut response and navigating through your comfort zone, and doing the thing - not only compounds in having a more influential intuition for yourself, but it helps ALL OF US. So thank you, in advance, for following your heart.

So here's the deal. If everything you currently have right now within your comfort zone is because your subconscious mind and ego got used to it, and has had plenty of proof it is "safe" for you, and there are things that are comfortable to you now that once felt like a rigmarole (hello learning to walk and talk, driving a car, riding a bike...), then you already know the uncomfortable can become the comfortable.

If you know that your thoughts aren't really your own, that your doubts are there to keep you in check within your comfort zone where the ego doesn't need to learn new tricks, and your inspiration is literally divine guidance from your soul, then you know you are safe to trust and follow your desires.

If the thoughts, beliefs, fears, or habits that come up for you when you're about to make a move towards your desires are really there to show you exactly where you need to grow in order to make the current-uncomfortable, comfortable; then you know you can take action anyway.

If you truly understand that your desires are 100% meant for you (otherwise it would literally be impossible to desire them), then you know that you have it in you to develop into the person you need to be to have, do, and be, all of the things.

Please keep in mind: You don't need to heal all of the

things and change all of the perspectives before you take action - the most effective way to shift and change is *in* the action. So create awareness around the thoughts that are there, and choose to act inspire of them.

You can do it. Your comfort zone, fears, and desires, are actually all on your side. Now, you've been waiting for the **secret to success**? Read on my friend.

Soul work: *Take a moment to bring awareness to the kind of thoughts, beliefs, and habits that come up for you when you're about to make a bold and ambitious leap towards your desires. Journal them and start to look at them from a new perspective to see if you can see how each of these relate to an area you can grow in as you step into the next version of yourself.*

INTEGRATION SPACE

Three

THE SECRET KEY TO SUCCESS

Look around you and look inside you. How many people do you think are settling? I will tell you: a hell of a lot of people. People are settling every day into okay relationships and okay jobs and an okay life. And do you know why? Because okay is comfortable. Okay pays the bills and gives a warm bed at night and allows one to go out with co-workers on a Friday evening to enjoy happy hour. But do you know what okay is not? Okay isn't thrilling, it isn't passion, it isn't the reason you get up every day; it isn't life-changing or unforgettable. Okay is not the reason you go to bed late and wake up early. Okay is not the reason you risk absolutely everything you've got just for the smallest chance that something absolutely amazing could happen. – Kovie Biakolo

A question that has baffled many over centuries is the question of what the key to success is. Some say it is most definitely hard work, others swear they are successful because they know how to take time off. Some say it's money; others say perseverance, attitude, hustling, generosity, commitment, doing what you love, stuffing crystals down your bra, calling on Archangel Michael, or chanting at the moon.

I believe all of these things have their place in some form or another, however, I think the true key to success is a lot more subtle. Something you may have not even noticed you do, something you may have overlooked, and something that anyone can apply regardless of their current attitude, circumstance, or stamina.

This key to success will support you in noticing your blindspots, showing you how you can shift and grow into a better version of yourself, and ultimately make the application of the previous list way more potent. It can be used to coach yourself when times get hard, to speed up the healing process, and to be a better version of yourself for the people around you. Yes, it's *literally that good.*

You want me to tell you the secret key already? Well okay, here it is.

Awareness.

Yes, you read that right. **Awareness is the ultimate key to success,** in my opinion.

What do I mean? Let me paint you a picture. Understanding what we covered in chapter two about the comfort zone bubble, you may recall that unless you consciously choose to change, you ultimately stay the same. In order to have things you don't currently have, it means you must move beyond what you currently know, and meet yourself at a new level. This process, more than anything, takes awareness. For things to change, you have to first be aware of where things aren't flowing as well as you would like. In order for anyone to change, it takes an awareness of what needs to change, and awareness in what you've done, (usually best seen in hindsight), and awareness around what direction you want to move in.

In order to change a belief pattern, you have to first become aware of what the belief is that isn't serving you. Then, you have to create awareness around every time you think this thought. This is the hard part... when you think the thought, even though you know it's not serving you, offering yourself grace and remembering your human-ness. You are allowed to take time to build new habits, and you don't have to completely eradicate old beliefs in order to start applying new, more empowering ones. Your success doesn't come from never thinking that thought again, however, if you're aware that you're thinking it, you now have the choice whether you buy into it, believe it, or simply choose a new thought.

Yes, it is actually that easy babe - no more overthinking, simply creating awareness. On top of that, I give you *full* permission to celebrate yourself every time you are aware of a thought, habit, or anything else that you are choosing to change.

Too often, you think that the shifts in your life, the magic, and the life-altering moments are the big things. They are not. They're the small things. They're the subtle shifts. Just like our inspirations to follow our hearts' desires come through small, seemingly insignificant signs. The same happens with the moments that will change your life. No angel is going to fly down from heaven with a jumbo harp to tell you that you're on the right path. You won't float and hear sirens singing when you've had a moment that could change your life. Most people, don't even notice it happened - which is why most people also stay that same. The shifts are so subtle, and they lead you to magic every time.

Take for example my client Emily. When Emily first came to me she was a self-proclaimed emotional mess. Only a few months prior she had broken up with her fiancé of six years because things weren't amazing (although they were 'good', what a brave thing to do), she was low in confidence, felt unhappy in her job, and felt hurt because something she perceived as a good attribute was often used against her when her boss would say she's "too nice." She knew I usually worked with helping people set up and grow epic soul businesses, but asked if I would work with her even though she definitely did not want to start a business. Of course, I said yes, because the way I see it, I help people become happier and more fulfilled, it just happens that a lot of them seem to channel their passion into a business, but it's not mandatory when working with me. During our initial consult call, I heard what she was saying, and I couldn't help but smile, because I knew this woman was larger than life. She had such a powerful purpose, incredible strength, and energy that is healing just when she's in your presence. I knew Emily would thrive in our coaching together, and I could already see her, CEO-style, running a business, and helping thousands of people; and I couldn't wait for her to see this for herself too. One of the gifts of a coach, and mixed with my intuitive abilities, is the ability to see someone where they could be, and not just where they are. And I knew there would be MAJOR shifts with Emily.

After just 3-4 months of working together, Emily was a new woman. She not only found that she didn't need to change her situation to feel happy, but could find a way to thrive exactly where she was. She also started to see herself in a whole new light. She had been given a raise at her job, been praised for her effort and posture in group meetings, and outside of her job she was learning how to see, love, and appreciate herself as a powerful, single women, ready to start dating again. On top of that, Emily realized that she had a gift that she wanted to share with the world, and started setting up her own soul business. She's had clients (who all praise her, of course), and is really owning her inner power. It's incredible to witness!

When she was first setting up her business as a relationship coach, we talked a lot about how she would facilitate those big shifts in her client's lives. What would she say, do, or offer them, that would change it all for them? So rather than letting her get into her head about it, we tapped into awareness and reflected on her experience. What was the shift that helped her go from feeling used in her job, to being given a promotion and raise? What was it that made her confidence go up? How did she tap into her inner power?

Once she started reflecting, she clicked. The major shifts, the massive changes, *the life-altering moments, were not big things at all.* They were subtle, small, and seemingly insignificant. She created awareness around what needed to change and, (most importantly), allowed the change to take place. And as she tapped into this awareness in her reflection, it allowed her to release the present resistance she was feeling around whether or not she could offer enough value to her clients. Double win for awareness.

The main thing that allowed Emily to completely transform in just a few short months is that she learned the power awareness had, and she was honest with herself about what was going wrong and where she had desires she had not previously admitted to herself.

You don't have to believe it's hard. You don't have to think it takes something huge that you don't have access to. You get to choose to let it be easy. So I want to offer you a new perspective: **It's awareness of the subtle shifts that will change your life**. Once you can embody this truth, all of the previous things mentioned at the beginning of the chapter - perseverance, hard work, days off, time management, crystals, oracle cards, cacao ceremonies - you name it, will not only become more effective, but the application of them will become next-to-effortless.

The one thing to keep in mind, and in awareness, is that there are two ways we can block ourselves from really shifting into who we need to be to have this epic success - even when we are aware of the importance of awareness (woah awareness-ception)!

The first hiccup people have is they aren't aware of, or put enough emphasis on, the small and subtle changes that are taking place. In order to really shift, we have to become hyper-aware of even the smallest shifts, and we have to consciously recognize them in order for our brain to pick up this new awareness and use it to shift in our future. If you want to steer clear of making this mistake, just celebrate every single time you are aware of something that can make you better, move you closer to your goals, or release old conditioning - regardless of how insignificant you feel it may be.

Secondly, and this one is kind of a gut punch so brace yourself, you are not being honest with yourself. Your ego is a little too inflated to even admit that you might not be going "all in" when you said you are. You might not be as focused on the good things. You might not be as far ahead as you're telling yourself you should be. And I get it, *I really get it.* Admitting to yourself that the reason things aren't going the way you wished they would is been because of you is a bit of a bruise to the ol' ego. I know everyone just wants to feel validated and good about what they are doing, and you *deserve* to feel good about yourself. But how about training yourself to recognize and celebrate your efforts, your commitment, your perseverance, your choice to show up, your awareness - rather than your idealized "results" you feel are the true marker of your success (cause spoiler alert, they ain't).

If you can learn how to be as flipping honest with yourself as possible - from admitting when there is something you could be doing better, realizing you truly aren't as fulfilled as you say you are in your j-o-b (or whatever it is you've been pretending makes you happy... you know, the "it's really not that bad" trick), and to owning those crazy-ass goals you know deep down you want to pursue. That's when the magic of awareness really kicks in.

Be aware of err'thang, celebrate it all, and be brutally honest with yourself. Got it?

One of the other aspects of awareness I have to touch on is the power of hindsight, and how you can shortcut your way to success.

One of the things about using awareness for changing yourself (and by changing yourself, I mean you are fucking perfect already - just allowing yourself to step into a higher version of yourself, mm'kay), is that often we really can't see what needs to change, or what may not have been serving us, until we can objectively look back in hindsight. Just like the story I told in chapter one about losing my Dad, I did not see the magic in the experience, until after I was #LivingMyBestLife. In order to really see how our actions are impacting us, we need to go through the experience, come out the other end, allow our emotions to settle (especially if it was a hard time, like a break-up for example), and then look back and create awareness around what worked, what didn't, what we learned, and how we can do things differently moving forward. Most people don't often do this. They act while their emotions still cloud their judgment, don't look for the lessons they could have learned - and this is why we see people making the same mistakes over, and over, and over again. We assume it's because it's hard to change (it's not), or that it takes a long time (which it can, if we always have to wait to go through a situation, heal, and then self-coach our way into learning the lessons).

The cool thing is that you can change, and you can change in an instant. The power comes from always looking back in hindsight and reflecting on who you've been, what you desire, what lessons you've learned, how you can do things differently, and how you can move forward in a more aligned way. Create awareness around what needs to shift, and move forward with this new knowing.

If you want to fast track this process, it's easier than you may think, however it involves a new person. Understand this, even the best brain surgeon cant give themselves brain surgery. This my friend, is where having a coach or mentor, comes in, or even someone who you know you can really trust their judgment, you look up to them and respect them, and someone who has your best interests at heart. Ideally, they are also excelling in the area you want to move into. When you have a coach one of the best things about it is they can see you where you *could* be, and they can offer you the awareness and perception shifts, without you having to go through them first. Of course, there are some things you may need to learn through experience, but so many things you can learn through osmosis.

When I first started working with my coach, I didn't do it because I thought she had some special answers I didn't have, that she knew secrets about success, or that she would teach me something profound I didn't know. I did it because I knew that spending time in her presence would allow me to calibrate with her energy. I would be able to tap into her way of thinking, her awareness, and her beliefs about life - so I would be able to align myself with that quicker than I ever could on my own. And guess what? It worked! No surprises there.

When you have a coach (or mentor, or whatever you want to refer to this epic person as), the true value comes in that they buy you time - the one commodity you can never get back. They speed up the process of change for you, give you a heightened level of awareness, and allow you to step into a higher version of yourself at an amplified rate.

Take for example Sam's experience. She is one of my clients who participated in my Soulful Business Academy (SBA) program. One of the things that I find with a lot of the newer business owners who join my SBA program is that they often find it hard to see the value in who they are (and I am sure you can relate to this too). It's the back and forth in the mind of: "Can I really do this? Am I made for this? Do I know enough? Will people take me seriously? Yeah but this, that, and those people have so much more knowledge than me, and are cooler, and blah blah blah, yada yada yada". You know what I'm talking about. [Pro-tip: create awareness around when you think thoughts like this, call them out for the BS they are and move the eff on with you extraordinary life].

As part of week-one in my program, I help the participants change the awareness they have around who they are. This continues on as a theme throughout the 7-week program, and it's designed to help the women see their value, build their self-belief, and really integrate their best qualities into their conscious awareness. When Sam first joined the program she was already in business and already had big goals for herself, but the comment she left me after about 6 weeks of working together in the program reminded me of what this was all for.

She said, and I quote, "You have made me love myself more - which is seriously one of the greatest gifts you could give someone, because from a place of love - everything changes." Talk about wow!!! Safe to say we were both a bit teary-eyed after this.

She pointed how that it was me who helped her get

there, but *really* what I was able to create was a shortcut for her, and the other women in the program, by creating awareness around their own awesomeness. They didn't have to go through years of application, to one day look back and say, "wow, I think I did good," (and let's be honest, probably still feel like they could have done more). Sam was able to create the awareness she needed to see all her beauty, believe in herself, and love who she was now, and in the moment, so that moving forward, as she said; everything changes. Towards the end of the program, and within the month after, she started hosting workshops which sold out, and skyrocketed her business income.

THAT is what awareness can do for you.

Awareness is the mo'effin' secret key to success you've been looking for.

Soul work: *Take some time to journal using the following journal prompts.*

Looking back on your life, where have you done really well? Where have things not gone to plan? What lessons have you learned? What are you currently doing that may not be serving you? What would be more empowering beliefs, habits, or things you could apply in lieu of the disempowering ones? What do you really desire?

Once your awareness on these areas of your life has been created, keep them in mind as you move forward in life.

INTEGRATION SPACE

Four

CHOOSE YOUR OWN ADVENTURE

You are free to choose, but the choices you make today will determine what you have, be, and do in the tomorrow of your life. – Zig Ziglar

Do we really even exist?

There is no way to know. What I do know is I'm starting this chapter off on woo-woo level 10 for a reason. To understand the science and psychology (#facts) I'm going to dive into with you during this chapter, I first want you to have a little existential crisis with me. As my old friend (#NotActuallyMyFriend) Elon Musk says, there is only a one in a multiple-billion chance we are not living in a computer simulation. That's right, the genius behind SpaceX and Tesla (and also the Almighty who founded PayPal), believes we most likely live in a computer simulation, so who knows what's really real.

Other perspectives say everything we are and everything we experience is a projection. Some believe it's completely virtual. Although I still get epic amounts of pleasure in assuming our existence is real, and not just a simulation, I completely believe that our experience in life is a projection of what is happening within us and within our mind. You see, we only ever see life through our own lens, so everything we experience is based on our interpretation, and that interpretation is based on our own beliefs and views of the world.

The other crazy thing to come to terms with is this: If you're a human, which I am going to go ahead and assume you are (#DidIJustAssumeYourSpecies #YesIDid #LoveAndLight), then at one stage, you were both a sperm and an egg. If you were at one point a sperm and an egg, that means you partially existed, alive, in two different places at once. Mind blown yet? And if you keep following your egg and sperm self back down the line of existence, at one point you would have begun in the very molecule that first ever existed (regardless of your "how we got here" - big bang, evolution, creation, simulation, etc., theory). If you came from the first molecule that ever existed, and so did I, and so did everyone else, we are all connected. We are all one. And you are everyone at the same moment that you are you.

So, how does all of this deep and meaning stuff tie into living a life of abundance, to building up the courage to pursue your goals, and to really having it all in life? Easy. It's all about the perspective and beliefs we *choose* to have.

We've all seen the comic with two people standing opposite each other arguing whether the number in front of them is a 6 or a 9. Who is right? They kinda both are. And this too is how life is. We see life in a way that is totally based on where we are positioned. Once we can begin to understand how to zoom out of our own perspective, combined with the awareness we spoke about in the previous chapter, we can re-wire brain patterns, see life from a positive space, and anchor in new, more empowering beliefs. What we are unlocking in this chapter is not only a deeper dive into seeing a new perspective, but also how you can choose to integrate your own, new perspective. It's pretty powerful stuff.

To ground you into this message even more, now that you've made it through the brain fuck from above, let's talk psychology. The things we focus on expand, meaning, whatever we pay attention too becomes more prominent and obvious in our life. There are so many things that can prove this truth, from the Law of Attraction and manifestation (which we will cover in the chapters to come), to straight up science. And here, I want to introduce you to the Reticular Activating System, a.k.a. the RAS.

The RAS is a super epic part of the brain that filters all of the information our brain is receiving on a daily basis so that we don't go absolutely crazy. Our short term memory only picks up about 4-9 'pieces' or bits of information from our environment at a time. The actual number of information your mind is picking up on is closer to 400 billion bits a second, and about 11 billion bits of that 400 billion are sent into the mind for 'processing'. Per second. *OMG face emoji*. Our brain only chooses to consciously show us what it deems as important and necessary for survival, *or* based on what we have told our RAS is important.

When we get emotionally excited or aroused about an idea, or repeat conversations around a specific topic often, our RAS picks that up and notes it as important. From here on out, whenever anything happens that supports this belief or view, whether it be to show us something we have been looking for, or to prove a point on something we believe, it will be sure to make us aware of it.

The classic example to showcase how the RAS works is bringing your awareness to a time you have wanted to buy a new car, a new handbag, or anything else. Suddenly, the car that you want that you've barely ever seen around, or a bag you only thought a few people had is everywhere! And the same thing happens when we decide we are failures or successes, weird or wonderful, scarce or abundant - the RAS will find you proof.

This is a HUGE thing to realize because once you can understand that you have a choice on what you get to focus on, and your perspective about any situation and your life is ultimately what impacts the experience you have, you can use this power to create a life that effortlessly calls in more magic, and even in the tough times you know it's amazing and all happening *for* you. Any so-called challenge or experience you encounter is actually a neutral experience. Have you ever thought about why someones "busy day" is the next persons "walk in the park"? Or why some people can't imagine anything worse than slow wifi (#IFeelYou), whereas others go through intense family feuds, and would rate the experience of frustration at the same level? What brings someone joy, brings another person agony, or vice versa.

Every experience is completely subjective to the person experiencing it. On top of that, there are no real good or bad experiences; the thoughts and emotions you have about a situation determine how you see the situation. That brings up the question, do you have the power to choose how you see a situation? Do you have the power to choose your perspective?

That's a big fat resounding EFF YES! The power of choice is so crucial to understand, but that doesn't, by any means, make it easy. Being able to choose to see a situation in a different light first begins with the awareness around your current perspective, and then consistently choosing a new way to look at the things happening to you or the things that have happened to you, until you rewire the patterns in your mind to naturally see them as “good” things.

I was reminded at how far I had come with rewiring my perspective with an experience I recently went through. In fact, as I sit here writing this segment of this chapter, I am currently feeling an immense amount of pain and sadness. I have been presented with a new obstacle that, although painful, has me in awe of my growth these past few years.

There was a time when for me when challenge meant I was a victim. It meant boo-hoo-poor-fucking-me. Now, I am not downplaying the emotions, pain, or struggle that come along with challenge. BA-LIEVE ME, I’ve been there. What I am wanting to bring to the surface and shift your perspective on is that you aren’t, and never have been, a victim. Nor will you ever need to be.

There was a time when I thought life happened to me. I thought that I was dealt a shitty hand in life, from being so “weird”, to losing my Dad, to my mental health struggles, and anything else I was not willing to accept or take responsibility for in my life. How wrong was I. It took me a while, but I finally learned I get to choose what I perceive to be true about life. Life is always happening **for** you. Not to you. It's happening *for* you. So, if every experience you are having is for you, then maybe even the hard times hold magic.

As I share this I remember when this idea was just a concept to me. It took time to start embodying it, but it all started with the awareness around choosing a new perspective. I now embody it, I have integrated it, and I know this is true. Because in the face of my current challenge, I allowed myself to feel and process my emotions, rather than trying to paint over it with a coat of false positivity. I communicated with my husband in an emotionally intelligent way, which has brought us even closer, rather than blame, guilt, or argue with one another. I genuinely feel gratitude for the experience, and trust fully in the timing of the universe.

Want me to tell you what happened already? Okay, here it is.

My husband, Nick, and I have been together for over 8 years at this point in our life, and we have had SO much fun together. Since we met we've had huge goals of creating success, traveling the world, one day having a family, and being able to enjoy it all.

At the start of December 2018, just a few weeks before writing what you are currently reading, we found out we were expecting our first child, and I don't think we've ever experienced more joy in a single moment together than that one. Up until then we always knew we wanted children, but it was a "one day in the future" thing. Even as we walked to a pharmacy in our country of travel at the time, Morocco (where they spoke no English, and we spoke no Arabic or French, it was definitely a L-O-L experience), to buy a pregnancy test, we were unsure of how we would react at the outcome. But as soon as we saw that second line on the pregnancy test showing "positive" we KNEW we were ready, and so flipping excited. Even though I was only 6 or 7 weeks, we had to share the news with our nearest and dearest, and the joy exploded through everyone's hearts who heard the news.

It was only a few days later when the cramping started, and a couple of days after that I started to bleed. It was such a whirlwind of emotions because all we had supplying us with info on what was normal in pregnancy was Dr. Google, where we could find just as many people with worse symptoms and a perfectly healthy pregnancy, as people with no symptoms who had lost their pregnancy. When it didn't get better for me, we booked in for an ultrasound. Again, in a foreign, third world country with very broken communication, to find out that I had miscarried.

What surprised me is the pain that I felt from this. It hurt. So. Fucking. Bad. Up until this point in my life, I had no idea how much I wanted kids, and this experience had burst that desire wide open. In this life, we all feel pain. No one in life is immune to it. However, the difference between me now and me back before I could embody gratitude for all things that happen to me is that now I *know* life is happening *for* me. I have the perspective that life supports me, and this allows me to always to choose to see a silver lining.

I choose to believe that only good things happen to me. That life happens for me. That my baby would soon be back. And even crazier, I had been intuitively told by my guides and two of my clairvoyant friends that this was meant to happen for healing, and I choose to believe this truth. What allowed my husband and I to go through this experience and see it as a good thing, rather than a devastating experience, is instead of seeing this as something that had gone wrong, or getting carried away thinking of all the reason why this could mean our future possibilities of pregnancy could look grim, we trusted that it's all good. We chose to focus on all of the good that came from it; we bonded more than we ever had (which is crazy considering how ridiculously close we already were), and we realized how excited we are to start a family. It opened up a new level of vulnerability between me and my audience when we shared the story, and I have no doubt my physical body also experienced a level of healing that it needed.

When I first started to retrain myself to see the positive aspects of life it actually started with the belief that everything happens for a reason. I wore this belief proudly and believed I was truly empowered by it for a very long time. In 2015 I was offered a perspective shift on this belief by a mentor, who challenged me to believe that everything happens for a *good* reason. I loved this perspective even more. I totally thought I had nailed it when it comes to empowering beliefs, until I had an experience in a Quantum Leaping session - where you tap into parallel realities where your higher self hangs out, super woo-woo and awesome, and something I take a lot of my clients through to help them align with the highest version of themselves a lot quicker. When I connected with my higher self, I asked her what her beliefs about life were, totally expecting she would definitely mention how *everything happens for a good reason.* I was shocked when she replied she did not believe that. When I then asked her what she believed instead, she replied "good things always happen to me," or as I have since reframed even further, "only good things happen to me." What this new belief allowed me to see is that my precious belief of "everything happens for a good reason," although helpful in tough times, alluded to the fact that "bad" things will happen and one day I would see the "good" reason for them. My new belief allows me to see that in fact, everything that happens to me is good - and holy potatoes has that belief proven itself since I chose to adopt it.

You see, it was being empowered in my ability of choice and choosing new perspectives that saved me in my darkest times. That forced me to look at life through a positive lens, and it can be all of these things for you, too. Of course, the process takes time, you have to rewire your entire mind before you can embody it, and you are allowed to give yourselves grace as you reprogram your perspective. But all it comes down to is a choice.

The power of choice is beyond empowering, and if you always remember that in any moment you have the ability to choose - your beliefs, your reactions, your actions, and so forth - you will live more freely, more abundantly, and with more fulfillment and personal power than you can currently perceive.

One of the practical ways to understand how this alters your beliefs and experiences is understanding the belief cycle. Each of us goes through a belief cycle that reaffirms our beliefs. It's either a vicious cycle or an empowering one. It starts off with the situation - which is completely separate from our belief or thoughts around the situation. The situation just is, it's not good or bad, hard or easy. Let's say for example you decide to start a business to pursue success and fulfillment - the situation is simply that you have a business.

The cycle then begins with your perception or your thought about the situation. Some people might say it is effortless to create success, whereas others may tell themselves it is hard to become successful, earning money in business is a struggle, or getting paid doing what you love is unrealistic. Remember, none of this is the actual situation, it is only the perception.

Next comes the emotions that then arise because of the thought. If you are telling yourself it is a struggle to earn money from your business, how do you think you would feel? Probably stressed, overwhelmed, exhausted, a little bit defeated, and from time to time feeling the work you're doing is pointless. Your RAS will be primed to see alllllll the reasons why it's hard, and you will feel it big time.

The next phase of the belief cycle is action. What sort of action would you take if you're feeling stressed, overwhelmed, and defeated with your business? Well, let's just say even when you're not procrastinating and putting your work off, you'd probably show up with an underlying energy of "this is hard and I'm stressed out." That energy repels clients, money and good things, it blocks receiving, and it ultimately ain't doing anyone any favors.

The actions you take then determine the results you get. I don't even have to ask what results you think you'd get if you're taking action from a space like that... you already know it's gonna be sounding a lot like crickets. As in nothing, nada, zilch, no real results worth mentioning. This result then cycles back up to the original thought about the situation and reaffirms - it is a struggle to make money in business.

What. A. Shit show.

But here is the crazy, wild, and exciting thing - you can choose to change the thoughts you think about a situation. What if, instead you said to yourself, "the more fun I have the more money I make." Wow! I mean, how good does that feel! If you change what you think, it'll change how you feel and act, and therefore change your results, reaffirming a new belief cycle.

Listen, everything in your life is a manifestation based on how you think and feel and what you choose to be true about your situation. So, if everything in your life right now is a product of the way you think about your life, what if you chose to think different thoughts? Yes, it's really that easy, you get to choose what you think, and in turn, experience.

Some beliefs you may notice rewire themselves essentially overnight, whereas others you have to work on over time, waiting for new connections to build up and grow in the mind. Regardless, your new beliefs will take hold at some point, and your old ones will automatically become redundant.

At the end of the day, you get to **choose** your beliefs. You get to choose how you perceive the world, and you get to choose how you show up. You basically are living in a simulator, and whatever you program is what manifests. Whatever you choose to believe is the most realistic outcome, is the one that you are most likely to experience.

Finally, to really drive the concepts covered in this chapter home, I want to talk about two life-altering things you can do to train your brain to look for the good in all things that happen, (thus make choosing your beliefs a little bit easier), and to also to speed up success in your respective area. Gratitude and celebration.

First is the power of gratitude. I know, I know, right now you're probably "ugh V, I thought you'd give us some real action steps to take! I've TRIED gratitude before." And I hear you, you may even be in a space right now where your finances suck, your relationships suck, your job sucks, and there is nothing to be grateful for. Well, guess what sugar, I ain't kidding you. If you properly practice gratitude it will change your flipping life. Firstly, it feels amazing to be grateful, and secondly, it activates the RAS, as well as the Law of Attraction (LOA), and will simultaneously rewire your mind to see more things to be grateful for, all the while actually calling in more abundant experiences. As you can see, I am all about the double-wins.

One of the most powerful times to tune into gratitude is first thing in the morning when you wake up, and right before you doze off to sleep. During this time your mind is the most malleable to new programming. This is why it is also my favorite time to visualize and meditate. As soon as you wake up in the morning bring your focus onto at *least* three things you are deeply grateful for. Maybe it's your bed, your pillow and your blanket, or maybe you go hardcore deep and meaningful about it. Either way, you are tuning into a frequency that immediately lifts your vibe, programs your RAS to look out for more things to be grateful for, which therefore shifts your perspective on life, AND it activates the LOA to bring in more good things to your life. How 'bout them apples?!

Secondly, and admittedly a harder one to apply than you may think is celebration. YES, celebration. As in throwing confetti in the air, having a spa day, shaking your booty to an epic song (I am SO all about Good as Hell - Lizzo atm), getting balloons, taking a bubble bath, happy dancing, and squealing with excitement kind of celebration. And for what? E-V-E-R-T-H-I-N-G!

Everything!

Noticed you were having a negative thought? CELEBRATE your awareness!

Chose a new empowering belief? CELEBRATE a new perspective!

Manifested an unexpected income? CELEBRATE how abundant you are!

Signed a new client? CELEBRATE that your energy is attracting people!

Something good happened to you? CELEBRATE re-affirming your belief that good things always happen to you!

Whether it is celebrating something you straight up

perceive as a good thing, or you're celebrating your awareness around things you're shifting in your life, we have to celebrate it all. How's it going to help you? I am mega glad you asked!

Too often in life people are so focused on the destination. Whether it be their goals, finishing their meal, or reaching the big O in sex, it is easy to forget about the journey. And secondly, most of us are so focused on the achievement of the 'big goal', that by the time we hit it, we are already focusing on "what's next." You hit your goal weight, yeah but you should probably tone up this and that. You smash through your income goal, well it wasn't actually that hard so what's the next level? You finish seven series of Game of Thrones, yeah whatever, when is season eight coming out?! Do you ever really take time to acknowledge or celebrate the achievement you have at hand? Or to even recognize how far you've come? Chances are, ya don't.

Other than the fact that it is fun to celebrate, the implications of smoothing over your accomplishments are actually huge when it comes to your growth. When you think about childhood, you got celebrated allllllll theeee tiiiime! The first time you wrote your name, everyone clapped and cheered for you. The first time you said "Dada," out came the camcorder (oh-emm-gee, did that just show my age, el-oh-el #TryingToAppearYoungAgainWithMyExcessiveUseOfAcronymsAndIronicHashtags). Pooped in a toilet for the first time, wow what a big girl you're being! Every single thing was celebrated. Then, as you get older (and especially for the ambitious,) you get so destination focused. Yeah, you might brag about your accomplishment quickly on Insta-stories, but only for a moment before you refocus back on where to next.

The reason we are celebrated so much as children, and parents are literally subconsciously programmed to fuss over their kid's seemingly insignificant accomplishments, is because celebration speeds up the integration process. To understand what I mean you have to understand that for things to get stored in your subconscious mind as a firm belief of who you are, or a habitual program, information has to go through three distinct phases.

First, information enters your mind, and as we have already discussed there is a lot of information. The next phase of integration is the experiential, or emotional brain. Not all information makes it into this part and it is only really triggered when your emotions are involved in an experience. This is why you tend to remember every meal you ate on holiday 5 years ago, and can't even remember what you had for breakfast yesterday - the holiday was full of new ways to look at normally mundane tasks, and an overall experience, versus just another day. When it is an experience with emotions involved you tend to be more attached to the memory, and then you are way more likely to reach the third phase; subconscious integration. When an emotional experience is repeated enough, or through a super heightened emotional experience, the information now moved into your subconscious mind, where it will now be integrated and easily become a part of who you are without you even having to think about it.

When you have amazing things happen, or you accomplish even the smallest of wins, if you don't take time to make it an experience and attach a ton of positive emotions to it, it won't ever have the opportunity to integrate into your subconscious. This means; Even when you make epic progress on your journey, it never really feels like you're succeeding. In a way you are working uphill as all of the proof of you succeeding hasn't become a part of your subconscious. This means; When you are faced with a new opportunity, the supportive beliefs and "proof" that you can succeed aren't as readily available, meaning you're way more likely to doubt yourself and give up easier.

This is also why obsessing over negative feelings about not being good enough, or how you could have done better, or coming up with one hundred and one reasons why you couldn't go for your goals isn't helping - it's literally just integrating this belief, meaning it is more readily available than the ones of you succeeding, which then means these beliefs or thoughts feel even more real when you are given the chance to step out of your comfort zone. Celebration is such a powerful way to shift your perspective on how you see not only the "challenges" in life, but also the opportunities. How about you just make it a whole lot easier on yourself and start making all of your beliefs around why you CAN and WILL be successful more readily available. How? By celebrating everything, duh.

Soul work: Choose to start believing that only good things happen to you - write it down and repeat it to yourself as often as necessary to really lock the belief into your RAS. From here, celebrate every time you notice yourself choose a new belief over a less empowering one - and I mean ***at least*** *a happy dance and self-high-five! Once you start seeing all the good things happening (that inevitably will) from choosing this belief, celebrate that too - even bigger! You better post your celebration on Instagram and tag me @violahug so I can celebrate with you!*

INTEGRATION SPACE

Five

WELCOME TO THE ABUNDANCE VORTEX

We don't create abundance, we are abundance.
We create limitations.

In your mind imagine a river. This river is the most magical river you have ever seen. It can be flowing through a forest, a valley, a desert, on the moon, or anywhere else you want to imagine this river. The color of the water is beautiful - you may see it as turquoise blue, or maybe your river is pink, purple, rainbow, or glittery. It's an epic flipping river in the most beautiful place you can imagine. This river constantly flows, is in unlimited supply, and is always there when you need it.

Regardless of where you are in the world, you can close your eyes and teleport to its location.

This is the river of abundance.

Abundance is the energy of unlimited supply; of love, money, time, relationships, food - you name it. When you are experiencing abundance in an area of your life you are in a space of knowing there is now, and always will be, more than enough. When you are aligned with abundance, you are in a state of knowing your souls true, unlimited potential. This is really the opposite energy to how most people live life - through scarcity.

Scarcity, on the other hand, is the embodiment of our human fears. It's when you've become detached from your unlimited potential and believe you are limited - by your situation, your skills, your resources, or anything else for that matter. It's the fear of there not being enough. It's the energy of greed, fear, hoarding, desperation, being overly frugal, withholding, and anything else that suggests a fear of, or belief that you currently are, or will, experience lack. Do you relate with anything of these? Chances are if you grew up on Earth you do.

In the world we currently live in it is likely that you, along with just short of 7 billion others, believe that it is more likely to experience scarcity than it is to experience abundance. Well listen up sugar, if you want to be living an epic as fuck life where you get to have it all without compromise, shifting to an abundance mindset is step one.

Tapping back into your visualization of the Abundance River, how most people access abundance is with the idea that this river is some place outside of themselves. It's the idea that abundance is something you achieve, receive, or when things are going well you have temporary access to. It's like you go about your life, and every now and then you prove yourself worthy and make the hike down to your beautiful river of abundance, dip your cup into its water, and head back to your current situation having experienced a brief moment of "abundance". Once this cup of abundance wears off you hope you're able to head back and refill your cup. Well, I've got news for you, the Abundance River isn't your cup of tea you keep forgetting about until it gets cold (I totally just reminded you of your cuppa, didn't I?!). The Abundance River actually lives within you.

The Abundance River is something you always have innate access to. It is your blueprint. Unlike something outside of yourself that you tap into from time-to-time, abundance is who you are. It is an electrical current that flows within you, and you don't need anything to be able to channel it. You hear that? You don't need anything to prove your level of abundance, because abundance does not depend on anything you acquire, your financial situation, your lifestyle, or anything else.

Abundance is a state of being. When you tap into the state of abundance, you also begin to amply its energy and attract more abundance in the form of experiences. The longer you stay in this state, the quicker you experience external forms of abundance. This is what I call the Abundance Vortex.

How do I know this? Because it was when I was having my worst time financially that I first felt what it was like to feel truly abundant. When, for the first time, I had tapped into my inner Abundance River. I didn't feel it when my business was booming. I didn't feel it when I was being given awards on stage. I didn't feel it when I hit new levels of growth. In fact, as much as I desired those things, when I experienced them all I could feel was lack. What if I can't do it again, what if I am not good enough, what if it all crumbles. Most of all I was so confused why none of it felt like I thought it would. It didn't feel enough, I didn't feel enough, and I was always focused on "what's next."

Before I knew it, my journey manifested exactly what I had feared. I feared I would run out of money. I feared I wouldn't be "successful" anymore (based on how I perceived success back then). My income plummeted, my business crumbled, and my debt quickly wracked up to over six figures. I was in pain over every dollar I owed, I felt like a failure, and I pushed myself to hustle my booty off to bring our income back up. The odd thing was that it seemed like the more I tried, the harder it became.

Through a series of events between 2015-2016, I

finally started to learn about the concept of abundance, and I heard it all differently than I had ever heard before. I started practicing tuning into my inner abundance, and suddenly I noticed things begin to shift. My husband and I had creditors calling us, our date nights now included backyard picnics rather than lavish nights out, and I hadn't bought new clothes in about 4 years. But it felt amazing. It felt joyful. I looked at my world and it lit me up, made me smile, and I felt a knowing of my true abundant state.

This knowing opened up the flood gates to my internal abundance, and before I knew it, I was buzzing around in the Abundance Vortex, and good things were happening to me everyyyyyywhere. Every day I felt abundant, and every day I experienced things that made me feel more abundant. When I look back now, those years of stress barely feel like a blip in the radar. But that definitely doesn't take away from the fact that at the time the transition was hard, and the situation was scary AF.

Remembering the concept of perspective I touched on in both chapter one and four, the main thing that allows you to tap into your inner abundance is knowing, believing, and trusting that you are innately abundant, and therefore good things are bound to happen. It is easy to feel abundant and praise gratitude to the universe multiple times a day when things are going well for you. Where it becomes a true test to your alignment with your inner Abundance River is when things seem like they aren't going to plan. Keep in mind, I am not talking about how you act in hard times in front of other people, at an event, or talking to your clients, I am talking about what is going in your mind when you crawl into bed at night and no one but you and your thoughts are listening. The real testament to your most aligned state is what happens while no one is there to witness it.

So, what do you say to yourself, about yourself, when you're by yourself? What fears, doubts, worries, or negative self-talk emerges when you're alone? If you have been calling in abundance, and haven't been feeling it, it's because these thoughts in these quiet times are derailing you from your own inner abundance stream. When you can begin to master these, your whole life will turn around.

Let me give you some examples from my own life. Let me take you back to when I was a wee 18-year-old spring chicken. This phase of my life was one of my most self-destructive, and I truly believed I was a victim to my circumstances, and that bad things happened to me (what a different world-view compared to what I have now!). I had a job in hospitality at a hotel and conference center and lived in the staff accommodation. I was incredibly good at my job. I was committed, I was always on time, and I gave 100% of myself to get things done better than what was expected of me (a work ethic I would later learn that only really benefits you when you're self-employed/an entrepreneur). Although I was this person at work, outside of my work I desired attention, validation, and I was dealing with the grief of losing my Dad only a couple of years prior [read: I was not dealing with it]. The staff quarters were filled with people who all seemed to have their own sets of issues - from older men unfulfilled in their jobs, or work-and-holiday visa travelers, to locals with gossip and drama. One thing was the same though. They were all there to party, do drugs, and drink themselves to blackout. On the daily.

Of course, I took part, and I totally thought I loved it. I would drink like crazy, wake up every day hungover, and when I was offered weed, I started smoking that daily too. One day a new girl came to live at the staff quarters and was (rightfully) appalled at the state of it. While everyone was partying I introduced myself to make her feel more welcome, and when she went to head management the next day to report the craziness happening at the accommodation, my name was the only one she could recall. I got dragged into a disciplinary meeting, got kicked out of the accommodation, and felt fucking furious. Why me?! I was the nice one!! I had done nothing wrong!! But everyone does it! How could I afford a new place to live?! It felt like an absolute betrayal and I could only focus on how things were going wrong. Of course now, in hindsight (as we know), me getting out of that environment was probably one of the best things to happen to me at that time. At the time though I felt tormented, and I tormented myself, and I was worried all the time about my income, my options, and my resources. Weeks of my life we spent throwing temper tantrums, crying, and getting drunk because I thought it was soooo cool.

Fast forward to a few years ago when I was really embodying the truth of abundance, and currently also being completely sober for over 3 years. Nick and I had decided to take a three month trip to the States, living off of our online business income that barely paid our current bills, and we just hoped it would all work out. Seems kind of crazy looking back now, but we have always been people to jump in the deep end and figure it out as we go. We relied on the fact we had a laptop we could work on as we traveled and explored, and as long as we stayed consistent with our work, we could maintain the travel. The first week we went on the most epic R.V. road trip from Las Vegas, through Yosemite National Park, to San Francisco, and down to Los Angeles. Only a few days into the trip, we noticed a bottle of water had fallen over right onto the laptop, and the laptop was completely fried. Our laptop, the one thing we need to keep generating our income while we were traveling for three months! And it was only week one. You'd think I would have freaked out, been worried, called my Mom to ask her to buy me a new one, but the energy was different because I already knew all about my internal Abundance River. I knew only good things happen to me.

As I opened up the laptop water ran out of it and the screen flickered a few times before going completely black. I stared at it equally blankly for a few moments processing what had just happened, folded the laptop shut, put it to the side, and said (and more importantly, believed) "I wonder what good will come from this." I didn't think about the laptop again for the rest of the R.V. trip. What was the point? Anyway, we arrived in LA and planned to stay with a friend who was in the middle of launching a business campaign and desperately needed some creative design work done. I offered to help, and as payment for my services, I was gifted... a beautiful MacBook Pro; newer, and with better specs than my old, broken, and wet MacBook. I smiled, thanked the universe, felt the abundant flow, and moved on with my life.

I could have easily tormented myself about this silly mistake, we could have ruined the rest of our road trip by focusing on this bad thing that happened, and I could have felt so much pain. But what was the point? I know both of these examples seem extremely different in the experience, however, both times my security was threatened, both times I had a choice in how I reacted, and both times it worked out for the better. So the question really is - if it's inevitable that it will work out in your favor anyway, why worry about it at all. You truly are an abundant being.

Redirecting your dominant energy from one of lack, fear, and scarcity, to one of trust, flow, and abundance, requires you to get really familiar with the differences in how those experiences feel. You probably are already very familiar with the feeling of lack - it's the tightness in your chest, the mind spiraling with worry, the sheer and all-consuming panic. But what about the feeling of abundance? If you really want to jump into your Abundance River you have to become aware of how abundance feels, and consciously choose to tap into that feeling at all times, or as often as you can remind yourself until it becomes your default setting. Think about times in your life where you did experience abundance, and how that felt in your body and energetic field. This feeling, however, is actually your default feeling, so once you start relaxing into it, momentum will pick up and you will soon be an epic magnetizing vortex of abundance.

The Abundance Vortex kicks into motion when you are truly feeling and embodying a state of abundance for a consistent period of time, so it's not just about feeling abundant here and there, but practicing and embodying this feeling at all times. It amplifies not only when you feel abundance in things you choose to perceive as abundant, like winning prizes or having a stacked-up bank account, but when you start paying attention to all of the small ways you are currently experiencing abundance; like the air you have to breath, the love in your life, and the joy in your heart. Remember - the more you tap into your inner state of abundance, the quicker external abundant experiences are manifested in your life.

Once you really start paying attention you will start to notice it. From finding a penny on the floor, to getting a hug when you are feeling like comfort, to your supermarket having a sale on toilet paper just as you run out of it at home. I can promise you, whether you notice it right now or not, there is abundance everywhere in your life. The more you notice it, and trust that you are an abundant being that the universe loves to provide with more and more goodness, the quicker this will become your reality.

Soul work: *To tune into the frequency of abundance, it's important to recognize where in your life you already experience abundance. Take 10 minutes to journal every memory you can retrieve of you experiencing, having, or embodying abundance. This brings you into the frequency of the abundance vortex and allows you to become familiar with the vibe of abundance. From here, remember the soul work from chapter three, and really begin to trust in that everything that happens to you is a good thing.*

INTEGRATION SPACE

Six

MANIFEST YOUR DESIRES, NOW

You don't manifest what you want, you manifest who you are.

Let's talk manifestation. If you're anything like I was, you probably think manifesting is something you have to get good at or be gifted in. Welllllll nope, just like with abundance living within you, you already are a master manifestor.

To clarify what I mean by manifestation, I am talking about a physical manifestation of something that was once in your mind. When you are consciously manifesting, you are bringing something that you desire into your reality. The thing to understand is that our energy is always manifesting, whether we know it or not.

In fact, every aspect of your life right now is a manifestation. It's a manifestation of what your energy field is attracting, and experiences to help you grow based on what you project that you want. On top of that, we don't just manifest based on what we want, we manifest what our vibe calls in. This is true for every single person. The question isn't whether or not you can manifest, but whether or not you can align with the vibration of the life you desire.

When I first heard this I almost resented the notion because I swore I only had positive thoughts and high vibes about all the things, and wasn't aware of all the areas I was being thrown out of alignment with my thoughts while I wasn't paying attention, (as we talked about in the previous chapter). Now, when you take on board this information I want you to be excited about what this means about your future potentiality, rather than beating your self up or overanalyzing things from your past.

We are always manifesting based on the energy that we exude, which is determined by the energy of who we are (what we embody), and what we believe most likely to manifest. Let's say I told you that tomorrow you would make a million dollars, or tomorrow you would make as much as you did yesterday - which would you be more likely to believe? Got it? Well, that is the one also most likely to manifest. So how do you become someone whose energy calls in their desires? Well, it is mostly to do with your energy, which is impacted first and foremost by how you feel.

Because of this truth, you can begin to understand how both worry and excitement are self-fulfilling prophecies. When you are focusing the majority of your energy on worry, your worries are the most likely to manifest. Alternatively, if you focus your energy on the excitement, possibility, and trust the Universe's plans for you, this outcome becomes the most likely to manifest. Becoming a master of your thoughts and your mind is step one to embodying who you want to be. To start this off I want to activate your RAS (from chapter four) by telling you to look out for every time you worry about something versus get excited by the good possibilities. If you notice yourself worrying, how can you turn that around?

One of the interesting things about the mind is that it loves finding answers to questions, and it can resist what it is told to believe. When we ask ourselves (our mind) things like "why am I so..." or "why is this so...," our mind/RAS goes to work to look for the answer. When this is something negative, it will do everything in its power to find data and information to support and affirm your negative belief. However, if this is positive, it will go to work affirming your positive belief. So, the one which is most affirmed or the most dominant belief is the one you will literally and physically manifest. When you are faced with automatic negative thought patterns, rather than telling yourself "it's fine, it's fine, it's going to work out," which your mind will probably rebuttal with, "no it's not everything is falling apart!" try instead swapping your "what it if doesn't work?" to a "what if it does?!" or "why does it work?!" How much more beautiful does that feel in the body!

Once you have more awareness of your thoughts, which in turn will impact how you feel, it's time to start focusing more on the things you would like to manifest. This is where visualization comes in. The subconscious mind can't actually tell the difference between what is reality and what is fabricated. This is why when you watch scary movies you are checking your closets for weeks after, why you cry in sad scenes, and feel love in your fave RomComs. Even though on a conscious level we are all "it's just a movie," our subconscious mind is thinking some whack shiz is taking place in our lives (which always creeps me out a little). This is the reason why visualization works. On a conscious level we know it hasn't happened yet, but if we allow ourselves to really feel the emotions of it having already happened, our mind begins to allow things into its "comfort zone," so they become easier to manifest into our reality. We suddenly act in ways we haven't before, we see opportunities we may have otherwise been blind to, and the universe unfolds its magic for us.

Alongside visualization, one of the other keys to embodying the feelings of what you would like to manifest, is to create experiences in your current reality that allow you to really feel into what it would be like when to are, have, or are doing the things you want to call in. For example, if you are wanting to feel swept off your feet and in love with your future soul mate, how can you create experiences now that feel romantic and loving? You may decide to buy yourself a bouquet of roses, and then after enjoying them for a few days, use the petals to create a rose petal bath, complete with scented oils and beautiful candles. If you want to feel abundant and wealthy, you might decide to set up a space in your house, completely DIY, that feels high vibe and luxurious, take yourself on a weekly spa date, or invest in a tea and work on your laptop at a local high-end cafe or 5-star hotel lobby to get in the vibe of wealth and luxury. Regardless of your budget, love life, health, or any other current circumstance, there are ways for you to create experiences now that allow you to tap into the energy of what you want to manifest. You just have to remember, you have to take the first step, and the universe will follow.

I remember when I so badly desired a long-lasting relationship, and I never seemed to get it right with my choice in men. I wanted it so badly, and I totally felt victimized as to why I hadn't met "the one" yet. This was of course until I decided to take radical self-responsibility and focus on how I could enjoy my own company for a while, and I set a standard for myself of what I was willing to accept in a partner. Unknowingly I had created my first 'manifestation list'. I made a list of all the qualities of, feelings, and experiences I wanted to have with my future husband, and was not willing to accept anything less. So at 21 years old, as well as getting "LOVE" in big block letters tattooed on my ribs (because I saw a video about the Japanese water experiments and figured if it works for water it would work for me too), I also looked at how I could become the perfect match for the soulmate I had written down on my manifestation list. I mostly did this on a subconscious level, but it all came down to the fact I was not willing to accept a standard lower than what I had written down, so I energetically wanted to match it.

Well, just a couple of months after my 22nd birthday, while boogie-ing in a bar with a Harry Potter scar drawn on my forehead, I caught the look of a man that would 5 years later become my husband. We clicked straight away, and as I casually-not-so-casually asked him questions about his life, from family history of diseases (yes I had this on my list, I want to create strong offspring okay - L-O-L-ing at myself right now), to if he played musical instruments, to if his straight teeth were genetic (they were), he fit everything on my list. But to be honest, at this point the list didn't even matter, because he made me feel exactly how I would imagine a soulmate to make you feel. I had manifested my dream husband, and it has been nothing short of amazing since the day we met.

So, what happens when things aren't manifesting? Firstly, as my mentor, Melanie Ann Layer, always said to me, the universe doesn't work on time, it works on alignment. Understand that just because something didn't manifest in the timeline you set for it, doesn't mean it isn't going to happen, or isn't currently in the process of manifesting. Stay on your path! Next, there are two main reasons why the things you desire are not manifesting, 1. Your thoughts and feelings are not aligned with what you want to manifest, and 2. There are shifts that need to take place in order for you to manifest what you are calling in. The first one is a real "check yourself" moment or something you may need a coach for. Because we are so close to our own thoughts, it's not as easy to see ourselves from a new or different perspective. Second, just because something you perceive to be the opposite of what you're calling in takes place doesn't mean your manifestation isn't working. It may simply mean it's time to prove you are ready to handle it. You may need to develop your emotional intelligence by going through an experience that triggers you, you may need to build your trust when things don't seem to be going your way, you may need to learn how to feel abundant before you can handle the riches that await you. But one thing is for certain, if you lose faith that life is happening for you and that all of these things are on your side, you will slow down the manifestation process, or completely block it.

The other thing to be aware of around manifesting is your language. It is important to talk about things you want in present tense (so as if they already happened), and about things you don't want in your experience in past tense. So if you are having money troubles and you say "I'm no good with money," - rephrase that to "in the past I have not been good with money". Whereas if you are wanting to manifest 10k months, rather than "I want to make 10k months," it's "I am so grateful I make 10k a month." Be very aware that "wanting" something only manifests more "wanting" of that thing you desire, not the actual thing - the universe can be very literal!

One of my programs I had created in 2018 was "Manifestation Mastery" which went over the 7 pillars of manifestation from language, to moon manifesting, understanding the universal laws, orgasmic manifestation, and overall how to become an embodiment to your desires. One of my personal clients, Montana, joined me in the program and totally started becoming an embodiment to manifestations everywhere, from running into famous actors, to free bus trips, you name it. However, even with all of this, she was having trouble manifesting large sums of money. She could easily manage small amounts, and there was always just enough to pay the bills, but with an upcoming holiday, she really desired to increase her savings by at least two thousand dollars. She decided to create a manifestation around this 2k and asked me for advice on the wording. Knowing the importance of how we "feel" when it comes to manifesting, I asked her to let go of how much she wanted to manifest and focus on how she wanted to feel on her trip - supported, and that she can enjoy herself and have fun. This is because sometimes we think we know what we need in order to feel a specific way, however, what if there was even more she could manifest, and she would be limiting herself with 2k. Or, what if it wasn't money she would manifest, but free accommodations, and additional support, so the money she already had was more than enough.

Montana instead focused her energy around how she

wanted to feel, and on day three of focusing on this manifestation, she got word of an inheritance she was not expecting and ended up manifesting over 10x what she originally wanted to manifest. How. About. That. Not only did she end up going on her overseas trip with more than enough dolladollabills in the bank, but she also manifested free accommodations and other incredible experiences on her path. The key for her was to bring her awareness to how she wanted to feel and let the universe take care of the rest.

What I want you to understand more deeply than anything is that you are a powerful manifestor already, and by focusing your energy on how you *want* to feel, and creating visualizations and experience in your current life that allow you to embody these things, you will become a magnet to the things you desire.

Soul work: *Get clear on how you want to feel in different aspects of your dream life. Now, create a practice and a point of taking part in regular visualization and activities that will allow you to feel the embodiment of your goals now. When you create these amazing experiences for yourself, be sure to upload some pictures, tag me @violahug, or email me the pictures! I would love to celebrate with you.*

INTEGRATION SPACE

Seven
LET YOUR FREAK FLAG FLY

People will doubt you. People you thought wouldn't. They will project their fears onto you. Fuck that. You're gold. – Unknown

Do you really know who you are? I mean really know who you are? Your deepest desires? Your likes, your dislikes, your body, your beliefs, your values? Chances are that unless you have actively worked on figuring that out, all you know is the societal-expectation-pleasing version of yourself. I'm not suggesting you're a people pleaser who doesn't stand up for what you want, however, I am extremely aware that most people don't think for themselves. You get passed on beliefs by your parents, teachers, society, you name it - and those beliefs eventually mold *your* opinions, personal beliefs, and who you think you are.

I'm sure you can relate to the feeling to striving for all of the things you need to be, all the courses you need to take, and all of the standards you have to live up to in order to call in higher levels of success in your life. Here is the crazy paradox, the more you strip that shit away and the more authentically *you* you are, the quicker, bigger, and bolder you will succeed. For-fucking-sure. Now I know that's a lot of cuss words for a little ol' paragraph, but I get fired up about this because for so long I didn't feel good enough, and the moment I gave myself permission to just be myself, I literally felt a weight lift off of my shoulders and I cried in relief. Just like me, you do not need to be anything but yourself in order to achieve wild-crazy-epic success, and in fact, the more 'yourself' you become, the easier it will be.

You are already hard-coded for wild-amazing-crazy success, abundance lives within you, you are a master manifestor, and your intuition and desires keep you up to date on what the next best step for your soul is. That nudge you feel saying you are meant for big things is totally on point. You were made for this. As you start to strip away everything that doesn't feel good, that doesn't serve you, that doesn't support you in feeling fulfilled and amazing in this lifetime (phew, what a relief right), your true guidance system can speak through you way more clearly, and you will take even bigger leaps and bounds towards your goals. This is like a subcategory of the Abundance Vortex that I call the Intuition Vortex, and the more we listen to our intuition, the louder, bigger, and better the messages are, and the faster you will succeed.

It's the story of the compounding penny. If you and a friend were offered the choice between taking one million dollars right now, or a penny that doubled in value every day for 30 days, which would you choose? Obviously, this story sounds like it's going to have a catch, so you're probably saying "the penny," even though the million is looking pretty sweet right now. Well, let's play this out, you take the penny, and your friend takes the million.

So day one, your friend books first class tickets to Hawaii and keeps you posted on her Insta-stories, and you have one cent. One. Freaking. Cent. It's okay, it's only day one. Day two you have two cents, day three you have four cents, and your friend just sent you a video of her in a limo sipping Cristal. Patience, patience, it's only day three, let's fast forward to one week in - a quarter of the way through the waiting period. Your friend has now flown first class (again) to Europe and is staying in a freaking palace, and you have... 0.64 cents... Cool, cool, cool cool cool cool coolcoolcool no doubt no doubt (shout out to any of my Brooklyn Nine-nine fans... Nine-NINE!).

Okay... Let's just skip past the one hundred and one snapchats from your friend sipping cappuccinos in Paris by the Eiffel Tower, her new Louboutin's, Gucci bag, and Burberry getup, and skip up to day ten. Surely something exciting has happened by now... eek, you have $5.12. Did you make the right choice? I dunno, but bear with me. Day 18 we can celebrate, you've made it over one thousand dollars with $1,310.72. Yeah, it's cool, but it's no comparison to the one million dollars and the helicopter tour your friend is on.

So when does this get fun? Day 21? You hit $10,485.76. Day 25 you surpass the 100k mark with $167,772.16, and you've totally stopped looking at your friend's stories by now. You are grateful for your 100k, but there are 5 days left, how much could really happen. Well, honey, this is where is magic really begins. On day 28 you overtake your friends million with a whopping $1,342,177.28!!! And at the end of day 30, you have $5,368,709.12 in the bank. HOW 'BOUT DEM APPLES?!

When you are living in the energy of a vortex, the rate at which things happen for you accelerates over time and the impacts compound. You may not be able to see the meaning of it from day one, however, the more you trust your intuition and choose to feel grateful and guided, the quicker and quicker success will be magnetized towards you.

Lucy, my very first long term coaching client was the perfect example of this. A couple of years before we connected she decided (read: was pushed by the universe) to go sober after suffering from alcohol addiction, a suicide attempt, and a host of other mental health struggles. She'd been on her path for a while and decided it would be a good idea to start blogging about it. During our initial consult, she asked me if I thought it was possible for her to turn her blog into a business, and possibly leave her job within a year. Her, having no business experience, no real background in entrepreneurship, and just a desire to help other women on a similar path to her own, she had no idea of the possibility that laid before her. Of course, with a big smile on my face, I said: "YES, YOU CAN!" I intuitively could feel her soul reaching out to me and it was showing me its desires, and I knew it was my job to bring them to the surface for her so she could know for sure that she was made for this.

One of the first things we worked on together, alongside all of the strategy of setting up her business, was about stripping back everything she thought she had to be, and listening to and acting on her intuition to take her back to who she really was. We tuned into her

Human Design (which is essentially an energetic blueprint of how your energy best interacts with the world), pulled up her deepest fears, and ignited a fire around her most desired goals. Lucy was totally on board with everything, and whether it was because I was there to support her, or because she was just so ready for change (or both), she took on everything head first with major courage - and it paid off.

About 2.5 months into working together she kept getting an intuitive pull towards Bali and the call to resign from her job for good. We talked about how her intuition knew best and that it was only up to her to either trust it or wait it out, and that moment she decided to leave her job. The universe, with its own sense of humor, really tested Lucy to see if she was really ready to go, in the form of getting offers for increased pay, fewer hours, and personal phone calls from the company CEO pleading her to stay. But she was fierce in her pursuit of her soul, and officially finished her job within the week, and stepped into entrepreneurship full time. By this point, she was truly living in the Intuition Vortex.

From there, she tapped into her own intuitive and clairvoyant abilities, got to know her personal strengths, and boldly showed up as she truly was. Before the end of the year, her and her husband moved to Bali, and they now live between New Zealand and Bali, have set up a non-profit, she has a booming coaching business, speaks and hosts at events all over the place, and is truly living her soul's purpose. All in less than a year. If that is not a testament to following your intuition and boldly being yourself, I don't know what is!

The reason Lucy had this success is because she fully owned who she truly was, underneath the conditioning she had experienced up to this point in her lifetime telling her who she should be. She let go of the idea she needed alcohol or substances to have fun, she decided she didn't need a job to create success, and instead created a movement doing what she truly loves and desires. And, she owned her journey every step of the way. Of course, you can't say that all came easy, however she was willing to take herself to uncomfortable places, she was willing to strip back the layers, and she met herself at a whole new level on the other side.

People crave authenticity. They crave vulnerability. They desire so badly because their soul wants to feel connected. So when someone is brave enough to show up in that way, people are magnetized towards them. If you can have the courage to be yourself, love your quirks, and let your freak flag fly, people will want to be in your energy. Success will come to you quicker than you could ever imagine. People will want to be in your energy so they can feel accepted in accepting themselves. How fucking powerful is that!?

It's worth mentioning that you stepping into your souls true potential won't always inspire the best in people. In fact, it's going to trigger the eff out of some people. They will resent you, put you down, fight you, or even worse, pretend that it's for your best. Now some of these people will most definitely be well-meaning, but it doesn't mean you should take their advice, like, ever. Here is the hangup for most soulful, heart-centered people following this bliss - when they have someone take a big steamy turd all over their ideas and inspirations they believe them. And you probably have believed way too many naysayers in your lifetime, otherwise, you'd be writing this book, not reading it (with love, you will get there, I'm totally celebrating you for being here right now)! What you don't realize is that other peoples reactions to what (or how) you're doing says so so much more about them than it does about you.

When we are born, and as we develop into the world, we are egocentric, meaning we believe we are at the center of the universe, and all things happen to and because of us. When we grow older and develop reason our conscious brain no longer believes this, however, a part of us could still be holding onto these ideologies. When I first started my entrepreneurial journey, heck, when I first started dreaming, I always thought it was me against them.

My positivity versus their pessimism.

My openness versus their close-mindedness.

My goals versus their skepticism.

I thought when someone doubted me it was a reflection of my incapabilities. It's not though. It's really not. Woman, listen up. When someone doubts you, shames you, cuts down your dreams, discourages you - they're reacting from the same space you're accepting it from...Themselves.

They think that because they don't know how they could 'do it', means that you can't do it. They think their fears are your roadblocks. They react from the place of insecurity within themselves. The truth is: *what other people think of you is none of your business*. What other people project onto you is not your truth. How you react however is on you, and part of your own growth journey.

If you are triggered by someone's reaction to you then, of course, allow yourself to feel and process the emotions. However, ask yourself - what about this made me feel that specific emotion? From this will come some super enlightening truths about what you can work through. If you're not triggered by it, then it's just water off a duck's back.

So when someone reacts in a non-desirable or unsupportive way, here is what you do. Send them love, and go for your big goals anyway. You might just be the person that breaks this belief cycle for them, too. Seeing you act despite fear may free them from the limitations they (and others) had placed on themselves. That is how you make an impact. That is how you liberate others while being free yourself. That is how you live a life of fullness. That is how you change lives.

<u>Soul work</u>: *Make a list of your quirks, your unique qualities, your best attributes, and really get to know who your soul designed you to be in this world. Decide on how you can show up even more fully this week in one of those*

areas. Maybe you will trust an intuitive nudge even if it's scary. Perhaps you will choose to talk about a spiritual belief that means a lot to you that you normally hide because of what others might think. Possibly *you will show up and launch the business or program that has been calling you, regardless of your families opinion on it.* WHATEVER *it is, I am here, I am with you, I believe in you, and I* TOTALLY *have your back (and so does the universe, of course)!*

INTEGRATION SPACE

Eight
YOU WERE MADE FOR THIS

"Become a millionaire not for the million dollars, but for what it will make of you to achieve it," – Jim Rohn.

This chapter might trigger you a little. It might make you uncomfortable. And yet, you are so ready for this work, so bear with me through what makes you uncomfortable. I am opening up space for you to fully admit to yourself that you want to be successful and rich AF, and that you love money! Something about it intrigues you, you want a lot of it, and you're looking forward to the day when everyday expenses just feel like pennies in your bank account.

Notice, I didn't say "you love money, but it doesn't buy happiness." Or "You love money, but you don't need it to be happy." Fuck that noise, I am not in the business of playing into the old paradigm perceptions of what it means to want, or to have money. I love money, you can too, and there is no need to justify how we are still good people and are grateful for what we already have. That is a given. As Jen Sincero says, you can love pizza and not have to explain every single time that, while you love pizza, family is more important.

Now granted, rich AF mean something different to everyone, and it may not be your main motivator, however, if you were really honest with yourself, you would know that money plays a role in the extent at which you can live out your soul's purpose. Wallace D. Wattles said it best in his book, "The Science of Getting Rich," when he said, "Whatever may be said in praise of poverty, the fact remains that it is not possible to live a really complete or successful life unless one is rich." What I loved about first encountering this statement is my immediate shame in the fact that I agreed, yet was scared that I would be seen as greedy if I admitted it. I would love for you to take a moment and really let the statement sink in for you - what is it triggering within you? Know that any reaction is okay from "I don't agree," to *yaaaaasssssss praise hand emoji*.

I am here to boldly challenge your beliefs around money, because there is way too much shit spun around about money, making people believe that they would become possessed with greed, have no morals, are cheats, scammers, or that there is somehow a lack of money, and you having more means someone else has less. And this is exactly my point, we need heart-centered, purposeful, #wokeaf, loving humans like you and I to succeed big time, so we can prove the old paradigm wrong. After all, money doesn't make you any of those things, it is simply an amplifier to who we really are and what we need to work through.

Money is simply an energy that represents a value exchange and is also an energy we create a relationship with. If you are wondering why your income isn't increasing, maybe take a look at your relationship with it. You say you need it when it's time to pay bills, but you say you don't want it when you're talking about how humble you are. You stress out when there is not enough, and say you don't have any when there is clearly some (even just a couple of cents) in your bank account. Is your wallet a mess with crumbled bank notes and too many cards, and you're too proud to pick up coins you find on the street? If money was a person, would they want to be friends with you? Would money wanna come over and visit on the regular? Or would they feel confused and disrespected?

Let's just imagine, money is your friend Dhanvi (random, I know, but according to Google it means a rich and wealthy woman). You tell Dhanvi you need her when you have a use for her, but you don't want her around when you're talking about how humble and self-sufficient you are. You stress out when she doesn't visit enough, and yet you don't acknowledge her when she's in the room. You treat her like nothing important and when she comes to hang out with you, you make her stay in a messy room full of hoarded junk, and you're too proud to say hello when you see her on the street?

...

Need I say more?! If we want more money in our lives, we should have a loving and respectful relationship with it. Be grateful for all of it, write love letters to money, don't talk it down, be conscious with how you spend it, and create loving space to accept more and more money into your life.

Here is where I want to take this deeper, and not only talk about money, but talk about success, and what it means to you. There are so many ways for you to experience success in your lifetime, and what I see for you is an abundant and holistic life where you have it all, no sacrifice, no compromise. To really sink into this knowing, and to share with you a little more on how my relationship with money truly changed, I want you to think about what constitutes success for you. What makes you feel successful?

Is it when you achieve a goal? When you get a good grade? When you're given praise? Yes, I feel you sister, I was this way too. When I first started my entrepreneurial journey I was just 23 years old, and I was ready to prove all the people that ever doubted me wrong. I was ready to succeed, and I was ready to finally feel validated for being myself. At university and school I had always worked on getting good grades, and regardless of the grade I got, I always had the feeling I should have done better. When it came to my business success I would set outlandishly huge goals, and when I achieved them I felt a sense of emptiness. Don't get me wrong, I had always felt positive and happy because regardless of how I was doing in life I was so proud of myself for at least doing what I wanted to do and stepping out of the box to follow my dreams. But I still couldn't quite figure out why hitting my goals felt empty. I would often have a really good week, hit a milestone, or get positive feedback about something, and notice myself spiral into an emotional low. Sometimes, right after I had seen apparent success I would cry by myself, or have an emotional outburst (sorry to my family and husband who I'd take it out on), not knowing what was happening. I thought happiness, joy, relaxation, fun, was reserved for the already successful, not for those still hustling their way to the top.

In my first year of business, I achieved every goal I set for myself, the biggest being a business milestone that would typically take someone 4 (or more) years, and grew a heck of a lot. Yet all I was focused on was, 'what's next'. Barely a day after I had achieved the biggest goal in my business so far, I set a goal two times the size to achieve in a quarter of the time. And because I was so used to getting everything I wanted, I figured it was inevitable, and spent my money as if I was already earning at that level. This is where the universe stepped in and said no more. No more ignoring your emotions. No more disrespecting money. No more settling. Time to raise the fucking standard.

After that, not only did I not achieve the goals I set for myself, I tanked it in everything. I booked flights for holidays I couldn't afford, funded our wedding, maxed out our credit cards, ignored our bills, ignored the creditors beginning to call, until we were six-figures in debt, and on top of that, my whole business crumbled and some weeks we would barely make one-hundred dollars. We had to borrow money just to pay our bills. It was during this time I remembered something I had once read, it was something along the lines of "your life will always match the level at which you are vibrating at." Meaning, the standard and level of your income, success, health, EVERYTHING, is set by the level at which you have grown too. My ego took a bit of a blow, but I knew that for things to change, I had to change.

I picked up my first financial self-help book, I applied everything I learned, and dedicated my year (which would become three years) to understanding money, building a relationship with it, and knowing how to manifest it. It was no coincidence that with my intention to truly build a relationship with money, I also had my spiritual awakening (and later my sexual awakening). These energies of money, spiritual, sexual, are one and the same, our default is a state of abundance, and as we tune back in with our soul's purpose and align with the power of creation that resides within us, we raise the standard for our life. When we do that, money, along with fulfillment, joy, and purpose, begins to flow more easily to us, and through us.

It was when I stopped seeking external validation and started to focus on feeling internally validated that I saw my beauty for the first time. It was when I was focusing on up-leveling myself, rather than seeking praise, that things started to change. When I made the association that money and success were so much more about the level at which I was ready to let myself elevate, making money became easier. Making money became easier when I decided I was ready to own who I truly am, and forget the expectations I thought other people had of me, which they most likely didn't even have. One of my favorite quotes that suddenly began to make sense to me was, "Become a millionaire not for the million dollars, but for what it will make of you to achieve it," - Jim Rohn. It's about who you are and who you become. It's about what level you are willing to allow yourself to grow to.

Each of us has a set point. We've subconsciously allocated how much love, money, happiness, etc., we are willing to let ourselves experience. You can imagine the set point as somewhat of a barrier between our comfort zone and growth. Once we go beyond that, we will either raise our standard and grow our comfort zone, or we will self-sabotage to reign ourselves back in. You see, we can't just raise one area of our lives, we have to raise them all equally. Like a wheel, each segment of our life must be at equal growth in order for us to ride along with ease. If only one segment of the wheel is extended, it would throw the flow off. This is why when you've come into large sums of money in the past, it probably didn't take long to get back to the income level you were at previously. This is also why over almost half of people who win millions and millions of dollars in the lottery go bankrupt within 3 years, and the rest are almost certain to be back at the same income level they were at before winning the lottery within the same time period. This is because if you don't up-level your money mindset and your energetic set point, you won't know how to handle it.

Have you ever had that? Where things seem to be going better than usual in your business, or your relationship, and suddenly you find that things go wrong or you make silly mistakes. I'm pretty sure this is where the saying "good things don't last," came from -

which is total BS btw, because when you raise your standard, the good things will stay. These are all indicators that you, my friend, are being faced with an energetic opportunity to up-level. You have a choice to create awareness around your self-sabotage, and more consciously treat the successes in your life with respect and awareness, which will set the standard for the rest of your life to up-level to. Or you can allow petty annoyances, or mood, or circumstances to pull you back down. You choose.

This is why before you dove into the conversation of money, I had to bring the other aspects of success to your attention - awareness, perception, the power of choice, you inner code of abundance, and your magical manifesting abilities. Money, riches, and wealth are a bonus. They are the side effect, the cherry on top. When you live life from the place of these 'success secrets', and you follow your calling (read: what makes you happy and brings joy and fulfillment), you will allow yourself to level up rather than self-sabotage. All you have to do is act in courage and build a relationship with money so it wants to flow to you.

The time has come for you to stop making excuses as to why you can't be, have, or do anything you want in your life. If you set the standard for it, anything you desire is yours. You can be equally successful in your vocation, relationship, parenting, health, or anything else you desire. So with that in mind, I am no longer available to listen to you make excuses why you can't be successful in your souls calling.

You may or may not have considered starting a business, non-profit, or some kind of self-created project. Or, you might already have clarity in where you are going and making tracks. What I want you to understand either way is that you are being called to these things for a reason, and you neglecting this path is a disservice to the world. As Marie Forleo says, "The world needs that special gift that only *you* have." I'm gonna go right ahead and assume if you are being called to read this book, you are here to turn your passion into a multi-six, seven, eight, and beyond, figure business.

Yes, that's right, a BUSINESS. A real life one. That impacts people. Creates influence. Inspires people. And changes the world. Now before you break out and tell me why you're not a techy person, salesperson, or businesses minded, you need to understand something HUGE. The successful business people of the 21st century are the soulful business owners. The ones who dream of a better world. The ones like you and I.

The age of "business sharks" has been and gone. Cheesy sales pitches, bulk emailing your contacts, copy and paste scripts, and competition has no place in our new paradigm. The ones who are here to build a successful business in 2019 and beyond are the ones who lead from the heart. Let me break down for you why.

Sure, there was a time when you had to compete with your neighbor. This was also a time where your business was limited to your suburb, town, or maybe your region - these were the dark ages before the internet. When the world was introduced to online connection, it revolutionized business. People could now market their products or services to more than just the word of mouth in their town, the folk reading the evening newspaper, or the people walking past their shop. In fact, with the internet, you don't even need a shop at all. It can all be virtual, and you can reach anyone in the world.

The rise of the internet also brought with it one

seeming downfall - connection. People weren't meeting people anymore, they were reading or seeing someones online persona. And when this is at the forefront of your connection with someone, your energetic senses are heightened - even if you aren't aware of it. When it comes to the virtual words, the energy behind your words speaks volumes, much more so than your actual words. With this, people stopped trusting advertisements and instead turned to consumer reviews - authentic words from strangers about their experience meant more than a companies billion dollar advertising budgets. Think about it, you would so much rather trust a review or recommendation, than a fancy website or billboard (and don't even get me started on infomercials).

This is where the soulful, heart-centered, intuitive entrepreneur steps in. For us, we are led by our emotions. We value connection. We genuinely want to change lives. And because of this, we are the most powerful people in the world at building connection - something your sleazy car salesman cannot do. We aren't afraid to be real, we show up with authenticity and vulnerability, and the world loves it. They crave it, they need it. People feel our vibes and they know our realness. This is the age of the heart-led entrepreneur.

You don't need to compare yourself with an outdated version of what a business person looks like. Yes there is strategy and energetic work to be done, but you can be guided by other soul sisters and brothers on your journey. All you have to do is show up as your true authentic self, and have courage when you're faced with opportunity or challenge. When you create a business from this space, it is more a way for you to channel your purpose - which will evolve and grow as you do.

Let your soul express what it has come here to do.

Allow money to amplify your ability to make an impact, allow yourself to enjoy all of the experiences money will provide for you. Stay centered in your purpose, and together we will change the standard. We will set a new tone for money. The more soulful, purpose-driven, heart-centered humans who create mega success, the more influence the people like you and I will have on the future of our world.

On behalf of your higher self and I, this is my call to action for you. Go on fellow Abundant Babe, there's a reason you desire riches, and it's because **you have been chosen to make an impact on this world** - make the most of it.

<u>Soul work</u>: *To raise your energetic capacity for wealth, this chapter's soul work is one part energetics and one*

part strategy. First, heal your relationship with money by writing a love letter to money. Watch your words around money. As you have learned from previous chapters, words create our reality; and be conscious of saying only loving things about money that would breed an incredible friendship. Secondly, start respecting money. This begins with you creating a tracking sheet where you can get to know your financial incomings and outgoings, and start tracking your income and expenses weekly. Remember, what we focus on expands.

INTEGRATION SPACE

Conclusion
YOU ARE AN ABUNDANT BABE

You are here to make magic in the world. The kind of magic that brings joy and fulfillment to your own life while making a positive impact on the whole freaking damn world. You were made for this, which is why you are here, reading this book.

You are the Chinese Bamboo, keep nurturing your goals, whether they are the first goals you're working towards, or you are already way down your path, because there is always a next level, a quantum shift, and more beauty awaiting you.

Remember your power. Know you always have a choice in your perception, your awareness, your reactions and actions. Abundance lives within you, you are powerful beyond measure, and when you come back to who you truly are, success is absolutely inevitable.

As I sit here having completely written my first book, having poured so much of myself into the pages, I am in tears. Happy, happy tears. In reflection of my story, I remember the part of me that didn't know how things would work out. That feared not being good enough. That felt like everything she desired was so far away. And I blinked and it happened. I went from barely paying my bills, to making more in the first month of 2019 than I made in all of 2017. I went from a desire to do more to an inbox full of messages about how I have impacted people.

And it happened in the blink of an eye.

It happened so much quicker than I could have imagined, and regardless of the time it took, as I sit here reflecting on this, every single moment of my journey has been worth it. It has all been magic, and it has all brought me unbelievable happiness.

The thing that gets me the absolute most about all of this is if I can overcome what I have been through, if I can train my mind to think and act like a divinely guided entrepreneur, if I can make this magic come through. **So can you**. I know this to my core and I believe in you so much.

For all of my days I will be energetically cheering you on, whether this is the only way we will ever connect, or whether we go on to work together in one of my programs, a mastermind, via my one-on-one coaching, or through collaboration. I believe in you. I want to see you winning.

If you would like to find out how you can work with me, I would LOVE THAT. Head over to www.violahug.com to explore your options, and feel free to join my free Facebook community, which can be found by searching "Abundant Babes: a home for the visionary," on Facebook.

I am so deeply grateful for you being here and allowing me to be a part of your journey. If you want to share what stood out to you most from the book, tag me on Instagram @violahug, or send me an email at hello@violahug.com. You could choose to be spending your time doing anything, and I honor you for being here. Thank you, I love you, and I am sooooo excited to see the magic you create in this world.

Remember, always; Abundance is your birthright. Your visionary goals will come true. Synergy creates magic. Energetic alignment creates physical mastery.

Growth is a journey to be embraced. High vibes and a positive outlook will change the world. Vibrant health is our default state. Integrity and credibility are a given. Success manifests in your life with ease.

And most of all, you are an Abundant Babe.

Vxx

<u>Soul work</u>: *Go make your dreams come true.*

If you found out you were dying how would you show up in life?

What new things would you want to experience?

What would you do differently?

Well, babe... You are dying.

We all are.

Bonus
INTEGRATION SPACE + JOURNALING PAGES

ABOUT THE AUTHOR

Viola Hug is a multi-passionate entrepreneur who has been ambitious in her pursuits ever since she started her first business venture in 2012. She often refers to herself as a "truth seeker," continually learning and studying things that interest her and offer more understanding on how to live a full and meaningful life.

Viola's journey includes polarity, from extreme hardships and trauma, to overwhelming fulfillment, joy, and success. This has given her incredible perspective and scope on what it really means to find purpose. She's well studied, holding a Bachelor of Science, various certifications and self-study in alternative practices such as Reiki, EFT, NLP, Human Design, intuitive gifts, manifestation, and more. Although, she attributes her success and knowledge to the courage she had to take leaps into the unknown, and trusting it would all work out.

As well as now being a published author, she is also the host of the Abundant Babes podcast (found on iTunes, Spotify, Castbox, and other podcasting hosts), and an Intuitive Business coach, working with clients both one-on-one and with her signature group programs. Her work is centered around bringing more purpose and self-belief into your life and channeling that into a multi-dimensional business that feels amazing and impacts the world. Find out more about how you can work with her on www.violahug.com (where you can always find free content and downloads to support you on your journey).

Travel is in her DNA, as she was born in Canada to German parents, grew up living in various countries, and going to thirteen different schools. From the age of 16 she lived in New Zealand, where she met her future husband (soulmate and twin flame) Nick Taylor, at the age of 22. She and Nick now travel the world as digital nomads, building their businesses online, and having so much fun.

Made in the USA
San Bernardino,
CA

58453872R00139